CROSSCURRENTS
PURSUING SOCIAL JUSTICE AND INTERRELIGIOUS WORK
SINCE 1950

CrossCurrents (ISSN 0011-1953; online ISSN 1939-3881) connects the wisdom of the heart with the life of the mind and the experiences of the body. The journal is operated through its parent organization, the Association for Public Religion and Intellectual Life (APRIL), an interreligious network of academics, activists, artists, and community leaders seeking to engage the many ways religion meets the public. Contributions to the journal exist at the nexus of religion, education, the arts, and social justice. The journal is published quarterly on behalf of the Association for Public Religion and Intellectual Life by the University of North Carolina Press.

The Association for Public Religion and Intellectual Life (formerly ARIL) is a global network of leaders, scholars, and social change agents who explore religious life, engage in intellectual inquiry, and lead ethical action in the world today. Their primary objective, especially through annual summer colloquia, the online magazine *The Commons*, and the scholarly *CrossCurrents* journal, is to bring together leading voices of our time to advocate for justice and to examine global spiritual and interreligious currents in both historical and contemporary perspectives.

Information for subscribers: Institutional print-only subscriptions are available for $250/annually. Institutional digital ($250) and digital/print ($300) subscriptions are available through Project MUSE.

A membership to APRIL includes access to *CrossCurrents* starting with Volume 58, 2008, though our partners at Project MUSE, monthly newsletters, early access to summer colloquium themes, a 40% discount on UNC Press books, and more. Membership rates are listed below:
Regular Membership with Digital Subscription: $55
Seminary or Student Membership with Digital Subscription: $50
Regular Membership with Print and Digital Subscription: $95
Seminary or Student Membership with Print and Digital Subscription: $90

We have a partnership with Duke University Press (DUP) for membership fulfillment and subscriptions. Agencies are eligible for a discount on the institutional rate. If you have questions about an existing subscription or membership please contact DUP Journals Services:
Email subscriptions@dukeupress.edu
Phone toll-free in the US and Canada (888) 651-0122
Phone (919) 688-5134
Duke University Press Journal Services, Box 90660, Durham, NC 27708

Postmaster: Send all address changes to UNC Press, c/o Duke University Journal Services, 905 W. Main St. Ste 18-B, Durham, NC 27701.

© 2022 Association for Public Religion and Intellectual Life. All rights reserved.
For more information about APRIL and *CrossCurrents*, visit https://www.aprilonline.org/

EDITOR

S. Brent Rodriguez-Plate
Hamilton College, USA

CULTURAL CONNECTIONS EDITORS

Rosalind Hinton
Independent scholar, USA

Hussein Rashid
Independent scholar, USA

ASSOCIATE EDITORS

Stephanie Mitchem
University of South Carolina, USA

Amanullah de Sondy
University College Cork, Ireland

Timothy K. Beal
Case Western Reserve, USA

Melanie Barbato
University of Münster, Germany

EDITORIAL BOARD

Fatimah Ashrif
Rumi's Circle; Muslim Institute, UK

Julia Watts Belser
Georgetown University, USA

Joy Bostic
Case Western Reserve, USA

Cláudio Carvalhaes
Union Seminary, USA

Judy Chen
Buddhist Council of NY and the American Buddhist Confederation, Canada

Robbie B. H. Goh
National University Singapore, Singapore

Henry Goldschmidt
Interfaith Center of New York, USA

Nikky-Guninder Singh
Colby College, USA

Scott Holland
Bethany Seminary, USA

Erling Hope
Artist, USA

Amir Hussain
Loyola Maymount University, USA

Robert P. Jones
Public Religion Research Institute, USA

Björn Krondorfer
Northern Arizona University, USA

J. Shawn Landres
Jumpstart Labs, Santa Monica, USA

Laura Levitt
Temple University, USA

Eugene Y. Lowe, Jr.
Northwestern University, USA

Peter Manseau
Smithsonian Institution, USA

Shabana Mir
American Islamic College, USA

Jolyon Mitchell
University of Edinburgh, UK

Diane L. Moore
Harvard University, USA

Harold Morales
Morgan State University, USA

Vanessa Ochs
University of Virginia, USA

Laurie L. Patton
Middlebury College, USA

Daria Pezzoli-Olgiati
Ludwig Maximilian University, Germany

Kathryn Reklis
Fordham University, USA

Christian Scharen
St. Lydia's Church, Brooklyn, US

Randall Styers
University of North Carolina, Chapel Hill, USA

Kayla Renée Wheeler
Xavier University, USA

Pamela Winfield
Elon University, USA

Homayra Ziad
Johns Hopkins University, USA

APRIL BOARD OF DIRECTORS

PRESIDENT
Stephanie Mitchem

VICE-PRESIDENT
Björn Krondorfer

SECRETARY
Pamela Winfield

TREASURER
Judy Chen

EXECUTIVE DIRECTOR
S. Brent Rodriguez-Plate

Julia Watts Belser
Eugene Y. Lowe, Jr.
Shabana Mir
Christian Scharen
Randall G. Styers
Homayra Ziad

PUBLISHING WITH *CROSSCURRENTS*

Articles: Each issue includes 4-8 main essays, generally on a theme, though we will also publish unsolicited submissions. If you have questions or are interested in submitting an article for review, please contact the editor, Brent Rodriguez-Plate, splate@hamilton.edu

Cultural Connections: This section includes book reviews as well as reviews of film, television, museum exhibitions, and any place we see religion meeting the public. If you have an idea for a review of any current cultural works, please contact Hussein Rashid hr@husseinrashid.com and/or Rosalind Hinton rosalindhinton@mac.com

We will occasionally publish poetry and short creative writing.

crosscurrents

VOLUME 72 : NUMBER 3 : SEPTEMBER 2022

SPECIAL ISSUE:
INTERRELIGIOUS DIALOGUE AND DIPLOMACY

ARTICLES

173 Editorial Introduction: Interreligious Dialogue and Diplomacy
MELANIE BARBATO

177 Diplomacy and interreligious dialogue: A generative model
PASQUALE FERRARA

196 Interfaith Dialogue and Healthcare Diplomacy during Covid-19 and Beyond: Parameters, Opportunities, and Constraints
NUKHET A. SANDAL

216 Putting Interfaith Dialogue on the Public Diplomacy Radar: Goals, Power, Strategies, and the Influence of Worldviews
JUYAN ZHANG

247 Bridging the Divides: Interreligious Diplomacy for Effective Peacebuilding
SHARON ROSEN

265 Interreligious Engagement and Political Theory: Between Virtue Ethics and Religious Humanism
MICHAEL DANIEL DRIESSEN

POETRY

287 Diplomacy
ABHAY K.

291 The Fire and Sermon
ABHAY K.

CULTURAL CONNECTIONS

297 Abu-Nimer, Mohammed & Renáta Katalin Nelson, eds.
Evaluating Interreligious Peacebuilding and Dialogue: Methods and Frameworks.
Reviewed by RICHARD MCCALLUM

301 Notes on Recent Books in Religion and Diplomacy

305 CONTRIBUTORS

MELANIE BARBATO

EDITORIAL INTRODUCTION
Interreligious Dialogue and Diplomacy

Interreligious dialogue is an umbrella term that includes many different goals and activities. It can involve discussions, art, big stages, or simply enjoying a meal together. If we want to better understand how interreligious communication works, it can be useful to take a more specific focus. In a previous issue of *CrossCurrents*, the focus was on interreligious aesthetics—discussing interfaith in the context of the senses rather than the spoken word.[1] This current special issue of *CrossCurrents* looks at another strand of interreligious interaction: diplomatic dialogue, the category suggested by Marianne Moyaert to denote dialogue between religious leaders.[2] This can involve big events, where leaders embrace, give speeches, and sign documents or the less visible, high-level meetings where negotiation and alliance building take place behind closed doors.

Religious diplomacy is increasingly perceived as an important factor in politics that can contribute to successful collaboration on a wide range of issues from containing local conflicts to addressing health crises like COVID-19 to tackling global climate change. While some see the dialogue of religious leaders as vital for bringing about a better world for all, others are more critical. Pope Francis wrote in his encyclical *Fratelli Tutti*, "Dialogue between the followers of different religions does not take place simply for the sake of diplomacy, consideration or tolerance."[3] The pope, arguably himself one of the key players on the stage of diplomatic dialogue, appears at least in this quote to see diplomacy as a surface phenomenon that interreligious dialogue should transcend. One frequently encounters even harsher judgments of diplomacy: that it is a political game, either the art of polite but meaningless talk or the proverbial velvet glove on the iron fist.

What then is the relationship between interreligious dialogue and diplomacy? There is no single answer to this question because both interreligious dialogue and diplomacy can refer to many things. The writers who have contributed to this special issue understand the term "diplomacy" in a wider sense that includes activities of both states and non-state actors. "Interreligious dialogue" is understood as respectful communication that addresses the other *as* a religious other. It is not seeking to motivate the other towards conversion but needs not be purely expressive either. Much interreligious dialogue has concrete goals: fostering joint activism for social justice, improving community relations (with the benefits for one's own community in sight), etc. Many of these overlap with the field of politics and diplomacy.

In that sense, both dialogue and diplomacy are related to power. This is sometimes neglected when interreligious dialogue is thought of in contrast to mission, as letting the other person be who they are, instead of trying to convert them. The power dynamics in diplomatic dialogue can but need not be a problem for religious communities. Another statement by Pope Francis, stemming from the time before he was elected to be pope and quoted by the British diplomat Nigel Baker, can be of interest here: "Religion . . . has to have a healthy power, insofar as it serves the human dimensions for the encounter with God and the fulfilment of the person. There has to be a power that proposes: I help. It is not bad if religion dialogues with political power."[4]

Involvement in diplomatic activity can enable a religious community to shape the world according to its values, whatever they may be. The category of diplomatic dialogue thus challenges the idea that religion should be private, without impact on the external word. It also raises questions like: What is a good or wholesome involvement of religious actors in politics, and what not? What cases are there that support the effectiveness of interreligious dialogue as a form of advancing interests peacefully? What is the potential and what are the limitations of this form of interreligious dialogue? To what degree do religious actors themselves understand their activism as "doing diplomacy?"

The essays in this collection reflect on the intersection of interreligious dialogue and diplomacy both theoretically and through practical case studies. The issue contains articles by academics in political science and communication studies as well as by those engaged in the practice of interreligious dialogue and diplomacy. In most cases, more than one of these labels apply to the authors.

Ambassador and Special Envoy to Libya, Pasquale Ferrara offers what he calls a generative model for interreligious dialogue and diplomacy.

While political actors have sometimes used interreligious dialogue as a means to advance their goals, this contribution makes the case for a quite different understanding of diplomacy as a practice in service of advancing interreligious dialogue. Such an approach recognizes that good interreligious relations are a valuable goal in themselves and cannot be replaced by short-term political initiatives intended to produce measurable outcomes in crisis situations.

Nukhet Sandal discusses the importance of religious diplomacy in the field of healthcare, including but not limited to COVID-19. Drawing on examples from different levels, she argues that religious communities are epistemic communities that have the legitimacy and networks needed to spread health-related knowledge and help implement healthcare policy.

Juyan Zhang has developed an Interfaith Dialogue Public Diplomacy Radar that maps and visualizes different practices of religious diplomacy on two axes, one of which indicates a spectrum from compassion to manipulation; the other measures the dominant use of narratives versus rational arguments. This radar serves to open a discussion on the internal diversity of diplomatic dialogue, the categories that should be employed to differentiate these sub-forms, and the normative evaluation that could be applied to them.

Sharon Rosen provides insight into the work of Search for Common Ground, a leading international peacebuilding NGO whose work also involves diplomatic communication across religious boundaries. She shares stories from her many years of working with religious leaders to build peaceful societal relations in general and advance concrete goals such as the protection of sacred sites.

Michael D. Driessen discusses theoretically rich concepts like "inclusive citizenship" and "human fraternity," which have been introduced by recent interreligious declarations and have caught the attention of both religious leaders and international policymakers. He reflects on some of the background sources of political theology that are advanced in these developments and argues that they draw on traditions of both "virtue ethics" and "religious humanism."

The issue also includes two poems by the poet-diplomat Abhay K., as well as a book review by Richard McCallum, and some book notes on recent publications in the field of religion and diplomacy.

I hope you will find this issue of *CrossCurrents* stimulating and enjoyable!

NOTES

1 S. Brent Plate, ed., "Interreligious Aesthetics."
2 Moyaert, "Interreligious Dialogue," 202.
3 Francis, *Fratelli Tutti*.
4 Baker, "Challenge of Pope Francis."

REFERENCES

Baker, Nigel. "The Challenge of Pope Francis: A diplomatic perspective by Nigel Baker, UK Ambassador to the Holy See." The Tablet, March 5, 2015. https://www.thetablet.co.uk/texts-speeches-homilies/4/581/the-challenge-of-pope-francis-a-diplomatic-perspective-by-nigel-baker-uk-ambassador-to-the-holy-see.

Francis. *Fratelli Tutti* [Encyclical Letter on Fraternity and Social Friendship]. October 3, 2020. https://www.vatican.va/content/francesco/en/encyclicals/documents/papa-francesco_20201003_enciclica-fratelli-tutti.html.

Moyaert, Marianne. "Interreligious Dialogue." In *Understanding Interreligious Relations*, edited by David Cheetham, Douglas Pratt, and David Thomas, 193–217. Oxford: Oxford University Press, 2013.

Plate, S. Brent, ed. "Interreligious Aesthetics." Special issue of *CrossCurrents* 68, no. 3 (September 2018). https://doi.org/10.1111/cros.12224.

PASQUALE FERRARA

DIPLOMACY AND INTERRELIGIOUS DIALOGUE
A generative model

INTRODUCTION

In the public perception, diplomacy is a traditional Westphalian profession, associated with anything from glamour to vanity to plotting, duplicity, secrecy, and obscure bureaucracy. As a result, diplomacy is usually understood through one of two prevailing paradigms: empty formality (parties and receptions) on the one hand, and on the other hand, instrumentalism and cynicism. Immanuel Kant was among the most authoritative critics of diplomacy. In his *Project for A Perpetual Peace*, he wrote that ambassadors are always ready to find ad hoc justifications for the futile wars of their sovereigns.[1] In more recent times, the so-called "realist" conception of diplomacy, based on power, interests, strategy has become a dominant narrative. As a case in point, the present tragedy of the Russian aggression against Ukraine seems to confirm this interpretation of diplomacy as either ineffective or as a utilitarian public function. However, it is equally possible to argue, symmetrically, that war begins exactly when diplomacy fails or plays no incisive role in international disputes.

In this article, my aim is not to offer a generic defense or "rehabilitation" of diplomacy, but rather to highlight one aspect of the connective power of diplomacy. In particular, my purpose is to argue that contemporary, reflexive diplomacy has the ability to engage with both religious and interreligious realities and entities in reciprocal discursive interactions. In doing so, I will move away from the ontological/empirical dispute about the nature and evolution of diplomacy, building instead on the phenomenological manifestation of new practices of diplomacy as they relate to religions as social, international, and transnational phenomena. As an introduction, I will elaborate on the tragic death in early 2021 of Luca Attanasio, the young Italian ambassador to the Democratic Republic of Congo, whose activism with religious organizations raises broader fundamental questions about ethics and diplomacy, as well as diplomacy "*extra muros*."[2] Elaborating on this specific case, I will then discuss two types of interrelations between religious diversity and diplomacy: religions functional to diplomacy (cases of diplomacy using or relying upon religious initiatives and religious networks) and diplomacy functional to religions (cases of religions using or relying upon diplomatic initiatives and diplomatic networks). I will conclude by introducing the concept of "generative diplomacy" as an interpretation of the underlying social texture that binds together the different manifestations of the connection between interreligious engagement and diplomacy.

FAITH, DIPLOMACY, ENGAGEMENT: THE TRAGIC CASE OF LUCA ATTANASIO

The public and media rarely think about diplomacy in terms of ethics, engagement, and outreach to religious organizations (beyond charitable events) until something unexpected compels them to look at diplomacy from a completely different angle.

This was the case with the brutal assassination, on February 22, 2021, of Luca Attanasio, the young Italian ambassador to the Democratic Republic of Congo. The diplomat was killed, along with two other people, during a field visit with a World Food Programme (WFP) delegation.[3] The shock the Italian public experienced was profound and reflected by events in the aftermath of this tragic death. The Italian thinktank Institute for International Political Studies (ISPI) dedicated its annual prize to Attanasio's memory;[4] the president posthumously awarded him the Order of the Star of Italy, while the Italian Ministry of Foreign Affairs named a conference room after him.[5]

Just a few days after his tragic death, a rather surprising profile of Attanasio emerged. He was not a "classic" ambassador, though his political and professional record was impeccable. In his spare time, he used to act as an institutional community organizer, engaging in impressive outreach to volunteers and non-governmental organizations active in the social field in Africa. To be sure, this kind of outward-facing activity is not new among diplomats, but Attanasio's case was unique because the discussion included a religious dimension.

The Community of Sant'Egidio, a well-known Catholic lay movement engaged in processes of mediation and reconciliation, recognized Attanasio. In an official statement, the Community expressed "its great sorrow for the killing of Ambassador Luca Attanasio . . . We remember him with affection, having met him several times in Rome and in

Kinshasa and having become acquainted with his great professionalism and humanity. In particular, Attanasio was passionate about the *Dream* project, through which Sant'Egidio in Africa treats AIDS patients. He was no stranger to all solicitation on social emergencies, such as support for minors in difficulty, from street children to those who attend our Schools of Peace . . . [He was] a sensitive man, committed to the common good."[6]

Two days before he was tragically ambushed and killed in the village of Kibumba, Attanasio visited the community of Bukavu, where Father Pietro Gavioli, a Salesian missionary, has been working for years. Attanasio used to meet with the small local Italian community, and he was very supportive of the educational programs managed by several Italian religious organizations.[7] Although their goals differ, Catholic missionaries and Italian diplomats have historically maintained a strong relationship, with both groups serving the Italian diaspora in different capacities since the country's unification.[8] Franciscan, Combonian, Salesian, and Scalabrinian religious orders have traditionally worked closely with Italian diplomats; more recently, members of the Community of Sant'Egidio and the Focolare Movement have established new ways of interacting with diplomatic agents, mainly in the fields of conflict resolution and interreligious dialogue.

Strictly speaking, Luca Attanasio was not a "militant for peace," as Scott Appleby defines the term. As a diplomat, however, he likely would have shared the conviction that "nonviolent religious militancy becomes politically effective over the long term only when it spans a spectrum of actors at different levels of society, all of whom are working in collaboration for nonviolent resolution of conflict and the building of stable political structures and social relations."[9] Interestingly, after his assassination, the Italian media engaged in much speculation over Attanasio's religious commitments. Attanasio's wife, Zakia Seddiki, whom he met while serving in Morocco, is a practicing Muslim. (Seddiki is also active in charitable causes of her own, having founded Mama Sofia, a nongovernmental organization that serves unhoused children in the Democratic Republic of the Congo.) Some people, including Hamza Piccardo, former spokesperson for the Italian Islamic association Unione delle Comunità e Organizzazioni Islamiche in Italia (UCOII), suggested that because of his marriage, Luca Attanasio had embraced Islam.[10] However, Angelo Gornati, the parish priest of Attanasio's hometown Lambiate, denied his "conversion" and stressed that Luca was a practicing Catholic in good standing.[11]

How are these episodes and debates relevant to the issue of diplomatic interreligious engagement? First, we must clarify that understanding whether Attanasio's diplomacy was influenced by his faith or if he simply believed in the morality of diplomacy is not a relevant question. Neither one's personal religious beliefs nor one's normative conception of diplomacy matter in this regard. What is important is the structural aspect involved in Attanasio's story. Several fundamental research questions arise from the analysis of his career. Does religion matter in the practice of diplomacy? When it comes to religion, should we distinguish between cases where religion is regarded as a *motivation* for diplomats from those where religion is merely a *contextual factor* for them? Is a diplomat's religious affiliation a causal factor pushing her/him to be more sensitive to social solidarity? How do interreligious context and encounters influence diplomatic culture?

DIPLOMACY TRANSFORMED

In our contemporary world, religion must be part of a diplomat's hermeneutical horizon. Religious literacy is an important component of any diplomat's conceptual and analytical training, as religion is no less relevant to peace and world order than issues of non-proliferation, trade, or development.

On the one hand, an informed understanding of religion can shed light on the common phenomena of attributing conflict and disorder to religious "fundamentalism," regardless of evidence suggesting that many so-called religious conflicts are rooted in power and material interests, and that religion is merely used as a pretext. (We can see this happening in the case of "religious" terrorism). Religious literacy allows diplomats to apply analytical tools to test conventional wisdom that paints religion as a source of intractable and drawn-out conflicts.[12] On the other hand, religion can also provide a set of normative concepts—such as peace building, global ethics, societal dimension, and contextual responsibility—that are key to effective diplomacy.

In order to better frame this discussion, it is necessary to focus on the substance of diplomacy's structural transformations. Luca Attanasio's tragic death brought diplomacy back into the public consciousness, where many people saw it as an engaging and demanding profession for the first time. There are four takeaways that can be gleaned from the comments and reactions following Attanasio's assassination.

First, if there is a concept that has become barely credible in diplomacy (due in part to the inflationary and empty rhetoric of international conferences), paradoxically, it is that of peace. This is even more surprising if one considers that peace is diplomacy's *raison d'être* as an alternative to war. Consequently, pursuing peace is (or should be) the ultimate goal of diplomatic service and practice.

In a world governed less and less by rules and increasingly influenced by the balance of power, diplomacy tends to be seen as a weak resource or a blunt weapon. The recent failure of diplomatic efforts to prevent Russia from launching a military attack against Ukraine have fueled political debates. This misfire corroborated the thesis that diplomacy is ineffective in situations of international crisis where there are threats of organized violence. According to critics, diplomacy is a tool suitable to be used only in times of peace and useless—if not harmful—in times of war. This is the central (and misleading) argument of many geopolitical and strategic studies approaches. The theme of diplomacy's futility has been raised on several occasions. In contexts marked by geo-strategic culture, the so-called "Munich stereotype"[13]— which likens diplomatic efforts toward compromise to appeasement of ruthless autocrats, powerful criminals, and armed groups—reappears. The stereotype takes its name from 1938's Munich Agreement, in which, according to critics, Great Britain, France, and Italy, failed to prevent the Second World War by yielding to Hitler and allowing for Czechoslovakia's annexation. According to this radically negative narrative (however incomplete and riddled with falsifiable counterarguments it may be), negotiation is counterproductive, encouraging aggressors to take advantage and pursue their own goals of power or conquest. According to this discourse, diplomacy itself should sometimes be accompanied by force (or the threat of it). Some analysts have tried to build a bridge between diplomacy and force, inventing the notion of "coercive diplomacy,"[14] which is, on closer inspection, an oxymoron. Equally inconsistent are the attitudes of states that declare that "all options remain on the table"[15] when negotiating with adversaries or enemies. Such declarations are metaphorically equivalent to talking with a loaded gun on the table.

The uncomfortable truth is that war and diplomacy are two discrete and opposite notions, not poles of a continuum that would allow for some combination of the two. It is a dichotomy, not a distribution. As Russia's invasion of Ukraine shows, states at critical junctures often behave binarily, being *either* aggressive *or* open to diplomatic settlement. Such a position is rather inelastic with respect to promises of coercion when based on the assumption of a favorable distribution of power or a convenient cost/benefit analysis.

The truth of the matter is that wars are usually started on the conviction that they will solve international disputes and confrontations more quickly and thoroughly than long and allegedly ineffective diplomatic efforts. However, several recent examples of military operations show that such an assumption might prove to be mostly wrong, with tragic consequences. We must not forget the protracted, costly, inconclusive—and even counterproductive—military actions taken against Afghanistan in 2001, Iraq in 2003, Libya in 2011, and Syria in 2013.

With regard to Afghanistan, after several years of "war on terror," as early as the mid-2000s, analysts started asking questions about the very possibility of a military victory against an elusive enemy in an asymmetrical conflict. Experts knew that al-Qaeda was somewhat distinct from the Taliban. Those who dared to hint at the prospect of negotiating with the Taliban were regarded as naïve, if not irresponsible. On February 29, 2020, after twenty long years, the United States came to an agreement with the Taliban and hastily withdrew its forces from the country in the summer of 2021.[16] In the end, the greatest military power in the world negotiated with the bad guys. This outcome was inevitable, and it should have been clear—at least to those who know anything about the region's history—from the outset of the military campaign that Afghanistan would maintain its reputation as "the graveyard of empires."[17] Without a reasonable and balanced political agreement that also include the Taliban (not the terrorists, of course), there would never be stability. That was exactly the conclusion of the military commands after two decades of war, thousands of military casualties, and many more civilian victims.

When Turkey decided to intervene in Libya's civil conflict early in 2020, there were some who advocated in favor of a similar Italian "intervention," as if Italy's constitution does not forbid using war as a tool for resolving international disputes (with the exception of actions on behalf of multilateral bodies, consisting largely of peacekeeping initiatives).

Many people think of military operations—especially those that take place abroad, in other people's homelands—as demonstrations of power. However, they typically end up revealing fragility instead and are unsustainable in the long term because of their political, social, human, financial, and reputational costs. We have seen this in Iraq, where the worst phase of the conflict began after coalition forces' supposed "victory" in 2003. Likewise, the eventual advent of the so-called Islamic State is considered by many analysts to be a byproduct of the destabilization of Iraq and the entire region (including Syria).

When conditions change, and when the weapons fall silent, those who favored political solutions over military operations in the beginning come back to the front of the stage. Diplomacy itself, in these cases, becomes a force. Broadening our perspective, it took a pandemic to make us understand that only with an infrastructure of international relations—of which professional diplomacy is an expression—based on loyal and open cooperation can the international community truly face global challenges. Relying only on national resilience and state capabilities may work in the short term,[18] but these qualities may be a cause of vulnerability in the longer term.[19]

Second, we need to reconsider the potential for bias in the relationship between diplomacy and ethics. Diplomatic ethics is not a question of personal attitudes, but rather one of the fundamental drivers of diplomats' training and orientation. Beyond the caricature of shrewd Machiavellianism often associated with diplomacy, it is a fact that in the international milieu ethics is rarely seen as a distinctive feature of a diplomat. The reasons at the root of this understanding of diplomacy can be found in the classic school of realism, which operates on the assumption that relations of power are ultimately the only factor that really matters in international relations. The truth is that so-called *realist* thinking often precludes one's ability to perceive *reality* itself. Is there anything more realistic and tangible today than listening to the "cry of the earth," recognizing and responding to the needs of the weakest and poorest? The actions of empowered individual agents like Luca Attanasio can make room for the idea of global justice, highlighting the persistence (and even growth) of growing inequalities.

Third, we need to reassess the relationship between diplomats and civil society organizations. Ambassadors, it is commonly believed, live in a kind of bubble, an artificial universe, separated from the real world. As an ambassador for Italy, however, Luca Attanasio's "mission" did not stop at the gates of the embassy. He went out and walked beyond the fences in an attempt to understand the realities of the countries in which he was stationed, not just official stories. This "open door diplomacy" is necessary for overcoming divisions between the public and the private; the governmental and the non-governmental; the secular and the religious.

Fourth, it is important to acknowledge professional diplomacy's great connective potential, for when conducted with intelligence and passion, it has the ability to foster empathy and trust. The structural changes occurring in contemporary world politics pose new challenges to responsible diplomats who, working in different operational fields and according to the different degrees of involvement and responsibility, must ensure a stable and constructive role for their respective countries in the new balances of power that are being redefined at a global level. Developing a conceptual map that allows for safe navigation of the new and changing world requires situational awareness and constant reassessment of the traditional parameters of the diplomatic function.

After all, Luca Attanasio decided to carry out his mission—to quote Pope Francis—"by initiating processes, not possessing spaces."[20] He believed in generative diplomacy, not perimeter diplomacy. In the last section of this article this concept will be explained and articulated in depth.

RELIGION FUNCTIONAL TO DIPLOMACY

There is general consensus among scholars that religion and diplomacy exert a mutual influence on each other, the latter being understood as a method of conducting ordinary foreign policy rather than a tool for conflict resolution. However, how this influence works is not always clear.

From a diplomatic standpoint, religions are usually considered essential symbolic narratives capable, in their constructive conceptualization, of bringing about mutual understanding in deeply divided societies. From this perspective, mobilizing different religions can be seen as a tool for finding a "zone of agreement" or overlapping consensus between conflicting communities.[21] Interreligious dialogue, in this context, becomes peaceful religious pluralism at work at the very core of societal cleavages. *Religions and interreligious dialogue, in a way, are understood as functional to diplomacy*. However, the very fact that religions are called to play a de-escalating role in confrontational situations could also imply a failure of diplomacy. For instance, in his recent encyclical *Fratelli Tutti*,[22] Pope Francis appears to be skeptical about the usefulness of diplomacy in post-conflict reconciliation processes, when there is a need for those who were fierce enemies "to speak from the stark and clear truth."[23] In these circumstances, he writes, "we no longer have use for empty diplomacy, dissimulation, double-speak, hidden agendas and good manners that mask reality."[24]

In particular, religions are highly relevant to processes of political reconciliation, even though critics require that "religious believers should only support those political policies for which they can provide 'public justification'—that is, a justification that does not rely solely on a religious rationale."[25]

The major religious traditions (Judaism, Christianity, Islam) can bring political reconciliation by enacting six practices: building socially just institutions; acknowledgment; reparations; apology; punishment; and forgiveness.[26]

That reality does not change the fact that in many circumstances, diplomacy sets the agenda and shapes the context of interreligious dialogue. Even in post-conflict reconciliation, politics usually dictates the overall picture (including cease-fires, provisional arrangements, confidence building measures, political/electoral process), whereas religious organizations attend to the societal context in order to promote de-escalation of rhetoric, recriminatory claims, and promises of vengeance.[27]

In a different domain, interreligious dialogue is gaining increasing relevance vis-à-vis the implementation of international goals, such as the 2030 Sustainable Development Goals.

The most visible role played by religions in the framework of global governance is connected to the G20. In particular, the G20 Interfaith Forum (IF20), created in 2014, engages the world's religious communities on global issues. Since its founding, IF20 has organized formal meetings that take place shortly before the annual G20 Summit. According to the mission statement proffered at the IF20 meeting held in Bologna in 2021, the Forum "brings important dimensions to the G20 process. It shares some features with other engagement groups but has distinctive aspects that relate, above all, to the widely diverse landscape of world religious communities. It serves as a place for high-level encounter and dialogue where faith communities and associated organizations can interact with public officials as well as with active scholars and civil society, building on the vital roles that religious institutions and beliefs play in world affairs."[28]

A special case of interreligious engagement connected to international events and priorities is the joint appeal approved by religious leaders ahead of COP26, the UN Climate Change Conference held in Glasgow in 2021.[29] The document, signed at the Vatican in October 2021, was the result of "months of dialogue between faith leaders and scientists" who came together "united to raise awareness of the unprecedented challenges that threaten our beautiful common home."[30] In search of "a framework of hope and courage," religious leaders and scientists advocated for intensifying international cooperation to "favor a transition to clean energy; adopt sustainable land use practices; transform food systems to become environmentally-friendly and respectful of local cultures; end hunger; and to promote sustainable lifestyles and patterns of consumption and production."[31] The Joint Appeal was approved by almost forty faith leaders, including high-profile representatives from across the Christian denominations, both Sunni and Shi'a Islam, Judaism, Hinduism, Sikhism, Buddhism, Confucianism, Taoism, Zoroastrianism, and Jainism.[32] The document was presented by Pope Francis to the COP26 president-designate, the Rt. Hon Alok Sharma.

In all of these cases the prevalent model of the interplay between religions and international issues is that of a "tool," as one can read in the Bologna IF20 summary: "Religions can be a precious tool if we truly want dialogue aimed at a better world."[33] This doesn't necessarily mean that religions are used or, worse, exploited by international actors and institutions to pursue their own goals. What is at stake is the *direction* of the interrelation, clearly starting from policy priorities to mobilize and involve religious responsiveness to social and political issues.

DIPLOMACY FUNCTIONAL TO RELIGION

A different approach is possible. Diplomacy can be instrumental in interreligious encounters, playing a facilitative role. In this case, *diplomacy becomes functional to religions*. Sometimes, religious organizations take initiative, rather than diplomatic institutions. Several cases can be mentioned in this context. In this regard, it is worth mentioning the story of the UN General Assembly resolution, approved unanimously on December 6, 2017, that proclaimed May 16 of every year "International Day of Living Together in Peace." According to María Fernanda Espinosa Garcés, President of the 73rd Session of the UN General Assembly, the celebration provides "a unique opportunity to recommit ourselves to our common principles and values of tolerance, inclusion and solidarity enshrined in the Charter of the United Nations. It offers a forum to further mobilize the international community around the culture of peace and dialogue, both within and between nations."[34]

The initiative behind the resolution began with a spiritual leader of the Sufi order Ba'Alawi tariqa based in Mostaganem, Algeria. The resolution's passage was the happy conclusion to a three-year global campaign initiated by the Association Internationale Soufie Alawiyya (AISA), led by Sheikh Khaled Bentounès, during the "International Women's Congress for a Culture of Peace" held in Oran and Mostaganem in 2014. The Congress then launched a petition titled "Desire for Peace" addressed to political authorities. After a diplomatic tour de force, Sheikh Bentounès succeeded in convincing the Algerian government (which had a history of persecuting Algerian Sufis) to submit the draft resolution to the UN General Assembly. Addressing delegates in New York on 6 December 2017, Sheikh Bentounès delivered a very inspirational speech: "No one can claim to have the whole; everyone has a part. Let us put ourselves in synergy; let us put our knowledge, our assets, and our will at the service of peace for all. Let us increase our investment in the culture of peace to extinguish the fire of hatred by the altruistic impetus of love. . . . I address this humanity of which each one of you is depositary, and humbly ask you to make this 'International Day of Living Together in Peace' a reminder of the preciousness and urgency of the reconciliation of the human family."[35]

The initiatives promoted alongside the International Day of Living Together in Peace (IDLTP) focus on eight themes: synergizing consciences; building bridges; advocating for sustainable development; reconnecting peace and spirituality; offering a global stage for world music and art; promoting gender equality and harmony; supporting architecture with a human face; and working for the creation of an Academy of Peace.

A remarkable point in this list is the idea of creating an Academy of Peace. According to Sheikh Bentounès, "its role will be to initiate and teach a pedagogy and a method to develop the Culture of Peace in all segments of society. It will bring together all the initiatives working in this direction. Each year, it will award an international IDLTP prize to an action for a better education in Living Together in the Culture of Peace."[36]

Another case study is that of the institution of the International Day of Human Fraternity (IDHF),[37] which is intended to provide an opportunity to highlight the principles and values included in the "Document on Human Fraternity for World Peace and Living Together."[38] The celebration was created with a resolution adopted by the General Assembly on December 21, 2020.[39]

That resolution underlines "the importance of raising awareness about different cultures and religions or beliefs and of education in the promotion of tolerance, which involves the acceptance by the public of and its respect for religious and cultural diversity, including with regard to religious expression, and underlining further the fact that education, in particular at school, should contribute in a meaningful way to promoting tolerance and the elimination of discrimination based on religion or belief"; encourages "activities aimed at promoting interreligious and intercultural dialogue in order to enhance peace and social stability, respect for diversity and mutual respect and to create, at the global level, and also at the regional, national and local levels, an environment conducive to peace and mutual understanding"; and acknowledges that "tolerance, pluralistic tradition, mutual respect and the diversity of religions and beliefs promote human fraternity." [40]

The first celebration of IDHF took place on February 4, 2021 and was sponsored by the UN Alliance of Civilizations, in partnership with the Permanent Missions of Egypt and the United Arab Emirates to the UN, as well as the Higher Committee of Human Fraternity. In this case, too, international institutions and diplomatic missions responded to autonomous interreligious initiative.

In this case, it is clear that the original initiative was taken by religious leaders (the Abu Dhabi Document on Human Fraternity) and then translated into an official international document. On the occasion of the second IDHF, on February 4, 2022, Pope Francis stated that "brotherhood means reaching out to others, respecting them and listening to them with an open heart. I hope that concrete steps will be taken together with the believers of other religions, and also with people of good will, to affirm that today is a time of brotherhood, avoiding fueling clashes, divisions, and closures."[41]

DIPLOMACY AND RELIGION: A GENERATIVE MODEL

The cases above seem to suggest that in both cases (religion functional to diplomacy and diplomacy functional to religion) the link between the two social institutions tends to be asymmetrical to the advantage of one or the other of the two realms.

In order to highlight the existence of a shared feature between these two different social and political acts (religion functional to diplomacy and diplomacy functional to religion) and going beyond the dichotomous approach that those two models entail, I would refer to a new social paradigm, that of "social generativity." Conceived and developed originally in seminal works rooted in psychology as "generativity," social generativity has been studied in sociology as a distinctive social phenomenon and an empirically observable process "composed of three crucial movements: bringing something new into the world; taking care of it; and realizing or handing it over."[42]

At the beginning of the process lies the desire of to transform a generic aspiration into a concrete realization. From this point of view, social generativity at this stage is a truly entrepreneurial force that may be put into motion by different reasons: it could be a genuine attempt to solve a social problem; a trauma (either individual or collective) that pushes the initiator to take a public stance; or the charisma of an individual who creates a new activity.[43] After the "generative drive" comes some form of institutionalization that is the result of "taking care" of the new creation. In order to reduce the risks of bureaucratization, generative groups need to focus on empowering others to carry on their work. Finally, generative social actors need to learn how to "release" their own creation, as "without releasing, 'letting go' or handing over—which means accepting loss of control—the entire generative process fails."[44] Releasing is a crucial stage of the generative social action, "a consequence of a realistic and positive decision about what we intend to leave as our heritage, being aware that we lose control over what we transmit, and there is something good in that loss, however hard it may be."[45]

A generative social action can be better understood as "'talking action': by pursuing goals that are not merely instrumental but meaningful, social generativity makes a statement not simply by using words but also by doing things."[46]

Social generativity produces effects, which are articulated along the three axes of intersubjectivity (authorization), intertemporality (durability), and contextuality (exemplarity).[47]

I believe it is also possible to conceptualize this peculiar relationship between interreligious dialogue and diplomacy in analogy with the recent sociological studies on social generativity, so that we can talk of a "generative" model of diplomacy. The model of social generativity can be applied to the interplay between religion and diplomacy, insofar as they engage in starting new processes (innovation, initiative, action), taking care of the new creation (institutionalization), and finally releasing it (when it can be continued by other social actors involved).

Diplomacy has necessarily become a "reflective practice that aims to ensure the sustainability, resilience, and mutual benefit to the international order or international regimes (trade, security, sustainable development) involved. In many circumstances, especially in conflictive contexts, diplomats become objective formulators of alternative scenarios to the conflict, often being bearers of three complementary concepts of peace: the minimalist one (peaceful resolution of disputes); the positivist one (respect for procedures even when peace is not the final goal, but mere coexistence); and a transformative one (with respect to the international order).[48]

It is debatable whether the new diplomatic agenda constitutes a *mere* change or a *transformative* change *in* diplomacy. This is certainly a debate of great interest, even though, in my opinion, it fails to grasp a central issue, namely the end of the separation between the diplomatic dimension itself and the great (transnational) ethical, civil, social, and religious issues that are difficult to understand. Of course, diplomacy remains an essential activity in intergovernmental relations, but it is equally undeniable that it is now directly challenged—in terms of responsibility and the ability to envisage sustainable solutions—by broad questions of equity, justice, and humanity that arise from the very configuration of current international relations. We commonly refer to "dividends of peace" in post-conflict situations. However, the same concept of "dividends of international justice" should apply for all actors in the complex and interconnected world in which we live. This is why talking about ethics and diplomacy has nothing to do with a moralizing approach to public life; it is rather an urgent exercise of diplomatic realism. A generative approach to diplomacy and interreligious dialogue may amplify and sustain the ethical goals of both diplomats and interreligious actors, avoiding any potential dispute in terms of primacy in agency and away from hegemonic temptation.

NOTES
1 Kant, *Project For A Perpetual Peace*.
2 Ragona, *Luca Attanasio: Storia di un ambasciatore di pace*.
3 BBC News, "Italian Ambassador to DR Congo Killed in UN Convoy Attack."
4 Ministry of Foreign Affairs of Italy, "The 2021 ISPI Prize Is Awarded to the Memory of Luca Attanasio."
5 Di Maio, "The 2021 ISPI Prize Is Awarded to the Memory of Luca Attanasio."
6 Comunità di Sant'Egidio, "Congo: L'ambasciatore Attanasio un amico appassionato all'Africa, grave perdita per l'Italia"; author's translation.
7 Il Resto del Carlino, "'Attanasio visitò la nostra comunità due giorni prima del tragico agguato' – Cronaca."
8 See Ferrara and Petito, "An Italian Foreign Policy of Religious Engagement: Challenges and Prospects."

9. Appleby, *The Ambivalence of the Sacred: Religion, Violence, and Reconciliation*, 122.
10. Agenzia Nova, "L'ambasciatore Luca Attanasio era musulmano, 'va considerato un martire.'" In response to Piccardo's comments, UCOII released a statement stressing the private dimension of religious choice and expressing condolences to Attanasio's family.
11. "Attanasio, il parroco: «Luca era un cattolico praticante, non si era convertito all'Islam.»"
12. I take the liberty of referring to my book, *Global Religions and International Relations: A Diplomatic Perspective* (2014).
13. Bottom, "Essence of Negotiation: Understanding Appeasement and 'The Great Munich Stereotype.'"
14. Levy, "Deterrence and Coercive Diplomacy: The Contributions of Alexander George."
15. Tierney, ""What 'All Options Are on the Table' With Iran Actually Means."
16. U.S. Department of State, "Agreement for Bringing Peace to Afghanistan between the Islamic Emirate of Afghanistan Which Is Not Recognized by the United States as a State and Is Known as the Taliban and the United States of America."
17. Bearden, "Graveyard of Empires."
18. See Fukuyama, "The Pandemic and Political Order."
19. See Parsi, *Vulnerabili: come la pandemia sta cambiando la politica e il mondo*.
20. Francis, *Evangelii Gaudium*, 223.
21. Rawls, *A Theory of Justice*.
22. Francis, *Fratelli Tutti*.
23. Francis, *Fratelli Tutti*, 226.
24. Francis, *Fratelli Tutti*, 226.
25. Philpott, *Just and Unjust Peace: An Ethic for Political Reconciliation*, 102.
26. Philpott, *Just and Unjust Peace*, 171.
27. Sampson, "Religion and Peacebuilding."
28. "G20 Interfaith Forum 2021: Summary."
29. United Nations Framework Convention on Climate Change, "World Religious Leaders and Scientists Make Pre-COP26 Appeal."
30. UNFCCC, "World Religious Leaders."
31. UNFCCC, "World Religious Leaders."
32. GOV.UK, "Holy See: Faith and Science: An Appeal for COP26."
33. GOV.UK, "Holy See: Faith and Science."
34. See the Statement by H.E. Mrs. María Fernanda Espinosa Garcés, President of the 73rd Session of the UN General Assembly.
35. Inandiak, "Marking the First International Day of Living Together in Peace, May 16, 2018." For elements of Sheikh Bentounès's spiritual message, see Bentounès, *Thérapie de l'âme*.
36. Bentounès, *Thérapie de l'âme*.
37. United Nations, "International Day of Human Fraternity."

38 "Document on 'Human Fraternity for World Peace and Living Together' Signed by His Holiness Pope Francis and the Grand Imam of Al-Azhar Ahamad al-Tayyib (Abu Dhabi, 4 February 2019)."
39 United Nations General Assembly, "Resolution Adopted by the General Assembly on 21 December 2020."
40 United Nations General Assembly, "Resolution."
41 Dicastery for Promoting Integral Human Development, "International Human Fraternity Day: February 4 the Second Anniversary."
42 Magatti, "Introduction," 3.
43 Magatti and Giaccardi, "Social Generativity: An Introduction," 20.
44 Magatti and Giaccardi, "Social Generativity," 22.
45 Magatti and Giaccardi, "Social Generativity," 22.
46 Magatti and Giaccardi, "Social Generativity," 18.
47 Magatti and Giaccardi, "Social Generativity," 25.
48 Sharp, "Who Needs Diplomats?: The Problem of Diplomatic Representation."

REFERENCES

"Agreement for Bringing Peace to Afghanistan between the Islamic Emirate of Afghanistan Which Is Not Recognized by the United States as a State and Is Known as the Taliban and the United States of America." U.S. Department of State, February 29, 2020. https://www.state.gov/wp-content/uploads/2020/02/Agreement-For-Bringing-Peace-to-Afghanistan-02.29.20.pdf.

Appleby, R. Scott. *The Ambivalence of the Sacred: Religion, Violence, and Reconciliation*. Lanham, MD: Rowman & Littlefield, 2000.

Il Messagero. "Attanasio, il parroco: «Luca era un cattolico praticante, non si era convertito all'Islam»" [Attanasio's parish priest: "Luca was a practicing Catholic, he had not converted to Islam"]. February 24, 2021. https://www.ilmessaggero.it/italia/luca_attanasio_funerale_islam_chiesa_ultima_ora_parroco_congo_africa_attentato_ambasciatore-5788540.html.

Il Resto del Carlino. "'Attanasio visitò la nostra comunità due giorni prima del tragico agguato' - Cronaca" ["Attanasio visited our community two days before the tragic ambush"]. March 1, 2021. https://www.ilrestodelcarlino.it/modena/cronaca/attanasio-visitò-la-nostra-comunità-due-giorni-prima-del-tragico-agguato-1.6078127.

Bearden, Milton. "Afghanistan, Graveyard of Empires," November/December 2001. https://www.foreignaffairs.com/articles/afghanistan/2001-11-01/afghanistan-graveyard-empires.

Bottom, William P. "Essence of Negotiation: Understanding Appeasement and 'The Great Munich Stereotype.'" *Negotiation Journal* 26, no. 4 (October 2010): 379–415. https://doi.org/10.1111/j.1571-9979.2010.00281.x.

Comunità di Sant'Egidio. "Congo: L'ambasciatore Attanasio un amico appassionato all'Africa, grave perdita per l'Italia" [Congo: Ambassador Attanasio a passionate friend to Africa, a grave loss for Italy], February 22,

2021. https://www.santegidio.org/pageID/30284/langID/it/itemID/40688/Congo-L-ambasciatore-Attanasio-un-amico-appassionato-all-Africa-grave-perdita-per-l-Italia.html.

Di Maio, Luigi. "Keenly Felt Memories of Attanasio and Firm Commitment for Truth." Ministero degli Affari Esteri e della Cooperazione Internazionale [Ministry of Foreign Affairs of Italy], February 22, 2022. https://www.esteri.it/en/sala_stampa/archivionotizie/interviste/2022/02/memoria-attiva-di-attanasio-e-fermo-impegno-di-verita-avvenire/.

"Document on 'Human Fraternity for World Peace and Living Together' Signed by His Holiness Pope Francis and the Grand Imam of Al-Azhar Ahamad al-Tayyib (Abu Dhabi, 4 February 2019)." The Holy See, February 4, 2019. https://www.vatican.va/content/francesco/en/travels/2019/outside/documents/papa-francesco_20190204_documento-fratellanza-umana.html.

Espinosa Garcés, María Fernanda. "Statement by H.E. Mrs. María Fernanda Espinosa Garcés, President of the 73rd Session of the UN General Assembly." General Assembly of the United Nations, May 16, 2019. https://www.un.org/pga/73/2019/05/16/international-day-of-living-together-in-peace/.

Ferrara, Pasquale. *Global Religions and International Relations: A Diplomatic Perspective*. Palgrave Studies in Religion, Politics, and Policy. New York: Palgrave Macmillan, 2014.

Ferrara, Pasquale, and Fabio Petito. "An Italian Foreign Policy of Religious Engagement: Challenges and Prospects." *The International Spectator* 51, no. 1 (January 2, 2016): 28–43. https://doi.org/10.1080/03932729.2016.1120955.

Francis. *Evangelii Gaudium* [Apostolic Exhortation of the Holy Father Francis to the Bishops, Clergy, Consecrated Persons and the Lay Faithful on the Proclamation of the Gospel in Today's World]. https://www.vatican.va/content/francesco/en/apost_exhortations/documents/papa-francesco_esortazione-ap_20131124_evangelii-gaudium.html

———. *Fratelli Tutti* [Encyclical Letter on Fraternity and Social Friendship]. October 3, 2020. https://www.vatican.va/content/francesco/en/encyclicals/documents/papa-francesco_20201003_enciclica-fratelli-tutti.html.

Fukuyama, Francis. "The Pandemic and Political Order." *Foreign Affairs*, July/August 2020. https://www.foreignaffairs.com/articles/world/2020-06-09/pandemic-and-political-order.

"G20 Interfaith Forum 2021: Summary." Bologna: G20 Interfaith Forum, September 12–14, 2021. https://www.g20interfaith.org/app/uploads/2020/09/G20-Interfaith-Forum-2021-Summary_final.pdf.

Inandiak, Elisabeth D. "Marking the First International Day of Living Together in Peace, May 16, 2018." 16may, May 15, 2018. https://16mai.org/news-posts/marking-the-first-international-day-of-living-together-in-peace-may-16-2018/.

GOV.UK. "Holy See: Faith and Science: An Appeal for COP26," October 4, 2021. https://www.gov.uk/government/news/holy-see-faith-and-science-an-appeal-for-cop26.

United Nations. "International Day of Human Fraternity." Accessed September 2, 2022. https://www.un.org/en/observances/human-fraternity.

"International Human Fraternity Day: February 4 the Second Anniversary." Dicastery for Promoting Integral Human Development. Accessed September 2, 2022. https://www.humandevelopment.va/en/eventi/2022/international-human-fraternity-day-february-4-the-second-anniver.html.

BBC News. "Italian Ambassador to DR Congo Killed in UN Convoy Attack," February 22, 2021, sec. Africa. https://www.bbc.com/news/world-africa-56151600.

Kant, Immanuel. *Project For A Perpetual Peace: A Philosophical Essay (1796)*. Whitefish, MT: Kessinger, 2009.

Agenzia Nova. "L'ambasciatore Luca Attanasio Era Musulmano, 'va Considerato Un Martire'" [Ambassador Luca Attanasio was a Muslim, "Should be Considered a Martyr"], February 24, 2021. https://www.agenzianova.com/news/ambasciatore-luca-attanasio-era-musulmano-va-considerato-un-martire/.

Levy, Jack S. "Deterrence and Coercive Diplomacy: The Contributions of Alexander George." *Political Psychology* 29, no. 4 (August 2008): 537–52. https://doi.org/10.1111/j.1467-9221.2008.00648.x.

Magatti, Mauro. "Introduction." In *Social Generativity: A Relational Paradigm for Social Change*, edited by Mauro Magatti, 1–7. Routledge, 2017. https://doi.org/10.4324/9781315163802-1.

Magatti, Mauro, and Chiara Giaccardi. "Social Generativity: An Introduction." In *Social Generativity: A Relational Paradigm for Social Change*, edited by Mauro Magatti, 11–40. Routledge, 2017. https://doi.org/10.4324/9781315163802-2.

Parsi, Vittorio Emanuele. *Vulnerabili: come la pandemia sta cambiando la politica e il mondo* [Vulnerable: How the Pandemic is Changing Politics and the World]. Milano: Piemme, 2021.

Philpott, Daniel. *Just and Unjust Peace: An Ethic for Political Reconciliation*. Oxford: Oxford University Press, 2012.

Ragona, Fabio Marchese, *Luca Attanasio: Storia di un ambasciatore di pace* [Luca Attanasio: Story of an Ambassador of Peace]. Milano: Piemme, 2022.

Rawls, John. *A Theory of Justice*. Cambridge, MA: Belknap Press of Harvard University Press, 1971.

"Resolution Adopted by the General Assembly on 21 December 2020," December 21, 2020. United Nations Digital Library. https://digitallibrary.un.org/record/3896456?ln=en.

Sampson, Cynthia. "Religion and Peacebuilding." In *Peacemaking in International Conflict: Methods and Techniques*, edited by I. William Zartman, 273–326. Rev. ed. Washington, DC: United States Institute of Peace, 2007.

Sharp, Paul. "Who Needs Diplomats?: The Problem of Diplomatic Representation." *International Journal: Canada's Journal of Global Policy Analysis* 52, no. 4 (December 1997): 609–34. https://doi.org/10.1177/002070209705200407.

Tierney, Dominic. "What 'All Options Are on the Table' With Iran Actually Means." *Atlantic*, August 10, 2012. https://www.theatlantic.com/international/archive/2012/08/what-all-options-are-on-the-table-with-iran-actually-means/260928/.

"The 2021 ISPI Prize Is Awarded to the Memory of Luca Attanasio – Ministero Degli Affari Esteri e Della Cooperazione Internazionale." Ministero degli Affari Esteri e della Cooperazione Internazionale [Ministry of Foreign Affairs of Italy], March 23, 2021. https://www.esteri.it/en/sala_stampa/archivionotizie/eventi/2021/03/il-premio-ispio21-assegnato-in-memoriam-a-luca-attanasio/.

United Nations Framework Convention on Climate Change. "World Religious Leaders and Scientists Make Pre-COP26 Appeal," October 5, 2021. https://unfccc.int/news/world-religious-leaders-and-scientists-make-pre-cop26-appeal.

Unione delle Comunità Islamiche d'Italia. "Rispettiamo il dolore della famiglia. Lasciamo che la scelta religiosa resti un fatto private." News release, February 24, 2021. https://ucoii.org/2021/02/24/ucoii-attanasio-rispettiamo-il-dolore-della-famiglia-lasciamo-che-la-scelta-religiosa-resti-un-fatto-privati.

NUKHET A. SANDAL

INTERFAITH DIALOGUE AND HEALTHCARE DIPLOMACY DURING COVID-19 AND BEYOND
Parameters, Opportunities, and Constraints

In March 2020, right after the COVID-19 virus started to spread around the world, media outlets featured an article that showed a Jewish and Muslim paramedic in Beersheba, praying together during one of their very few breaks while responding to COVID patients. The article quickly became popular on social media as it displayed an uplifting example of interfaith co-existence at a very difficult time for healthcare workers. Zoher Abu Jama, the Muslim paramedic, said, "I believe that God will help us and we will get through this. We should all pray to God to get us through this, and we will get through this world crisis," expressing a sentiment that his Jewish partner, Avraham Mintz, shared.[1] The pandemic created a healthcare crisis with a high toll on physical and mental health. During these difficult times, daily partnerships among ordinary people from different faith traditions (like the one between Abu Jama and Mintz), as well as the initiatives that brought the religious leaders and organizations together with public health professionals, attracted attention.

Partly inspired by the uptick in interfaith projects and communications during the pandemic, this article looks at instances and dynamics of interfaith cooperation and diplomacy to tackle the various health crises such COVID and HIV/AIDS. There are many issues that benefit from interfaith diplomacy, ranging from peacebuilding in conflict-laden areas to responses to pressing challenges like climate change. Health and healthcare have quickly climbed to the top of that list, especially given the strain the pandemic has put on resources and infrastructure around the world. In this article, I first provide a theoretical framework to account for the role of religious actors in healthcare. Then, I turn to investigating the platforms and dynamics of religious epistemic connections in health and healthcare within the context of interfaith initiatives and diplomacy, including recent examples involving responses to the pandemic. Interfaith initiatives are not without their challenges and there are many questions about their future; the third section looks at those dimensions.

RELIGIOUS ACTORS AS EPISTEMIC COMMUNITIES OF HEALTH

There is an established literature on religion and health.[2] The literature on interfaith initiatives and diplomacy on healthcare, however, is still very limited. In a step toward filling this gap, I argue that faith-based actors—including religious leaders—constitute a distinct community of practice and expertise when it comes to health and healthcare. In other words, they are epistemic communities and can be described as networks "of professionals with recognized expertise and competence in a particular domain and an authoritative claim to policy-relevant knowledge within that domain or issue-area."[3] Epistemic communities constitute a subset of "communities of practice."[4] Adler gives diplomats "sharing a diplomatic culture, common values, and interests that are intrinsic to their practice" as an example of a community of practice, whereas Cross describes the European Diplomatic Corps as an "epistemic community."[5] In this article, similarly, I recognize that religious actors form communities of practice, yet also emphasize the importance of their expertise, competence, and knowledge production, situating them in the subcategory of epistemic communities. I use "epistemic communities" instead of "communities of practice" because the latter is implied in the former, but epistemic communities have a distinct dimension of knowledge production that not every community of practice has.

The epistemic community framework has already been used to explain faith-based actors' activities in areas other than health. I, for example, have argued elsewhere that religious actors are uniquely situated to make a change in a given situation due to their religious expertise, shared norms and understanding, as well as their standing in their communities, and these features qualify them as epistemic communities in conflict transformation.[6] This article argues that religious actors can constitute critical epistemic communities in healthcare as well—especially when they collaborate with health professionals and engage in interfaith dialogue and diplomacy—for four main reasons.

First, religious actors can speak to very specific values, texts, and interpretations. Hall, Koenig, and Meador describe religion as a cultural-linguistic system with its own approaches to health, rather than as a type of "optional" and "less trustworthy" knowledge that "may be added to the foundation built by reason and empiricism."[7] Following this description, it is inevitable that religious actors and leaders are needed since they "speak" this language and can help believers make sense of relevant developments and plans. Some people might even be more receptive to religious messages than to scientific knowledge.[8] The former sometimes prescribes what the borders of the latter should be. To take it one step further, differences across religions might be smaller than the difference between religious and secular approaches in certain settings, which paves the way for interfaith dialogue. In Israel, for example, the opening of a medical school was delayed due to unfavorable Jewish and Islamic views on autopsies.[9]

Second, as we have observed with COVID, religious actors can be seen by some as more trustworthy than politicians and scientists. There is occasional resistance to healthcare advice due to the distrust of government sponsored campaigns. In Liberia, for example, Ebola was initially seen as a government scam to attract foreign aid.[10] Conspiracy theories about Zika prevented early measures from being enacted in Brazil.[11] Some communities might see scientific knowledge as politicized and untrustworthy for various reasons.[12] This is also the case for various marginalized communities, whose bodies have historically been either ignored or abused in the name of medicine or science. Religious epistemic communities of health can help decolonize biomedical practices and recognize the knowledge claims of marginalized and indigenous communities in their medical decision-making.[13]

Third, religious leaders have connections and reach that scientists or health professionals might not always have. To illustrate, Ottawa Public Health's research found that "Ottawa's African, Black and Caribbean communities indicated faith leaders were among the first contacts they would turn to for help with mental health issues," which then led Ottawa Public Health to train faith leaders on dealing with the members of their communities who need mental health support.[14]

Fourth, although this article defines health relatively narrowly, religious initiatives—including interfaith diplomacy—address health holistically, focusing also on structural issues related to poverty, inequality, and climate change. Religious actors do not specialize in a narrow segment of wellness; due to their vocation, many see human life and its interaction with the rest of the world from a more integrated lens. In the Glasgow Multifaith Declaration, for example, senior religious leaders in the United Kingdom committed to working together in responding to climate change; they vowed to hold governments and businesses accountable in pursuing "science-based targets that are aligned with a healthy, resilient, zero-emissions future."[15]

There are also an increasing number of interfaith initiatives focusing on mental health. Ramsey-Lucas, who served as director of interfaith engagement at the American Association of People with Disabilities, points to the need for sustained channels of communication and partnerships between psychiatrists and clergy and underlines the existing interfaith initiatives that focus on mental health, such as the Interfaith Network on Mental Illness and Pathways to Promise. In Georgia, the Community Health Interfaith Partnership (CHIP) offers mental health first-aid courses to religious leaders and works towards what it calls "compassionate congregations," which it describe as "faith communities where awareness, welcome, support, and spiritual care for individuals and families facing mental illness are provided."[16] Action Dignity, another interfaith initiative based in Alberta, Canada, has identified possible actions such as forming "faith connectors who can speak various languages"; "cross visits among faith communities to share and learn"; "destigmatizing seeking help"; and organizing "interfaith orientation[s] on mental health."[17]

Due to their unique positions in society, faith-based actors, including religious leaders, are well-situated to collaborate both with each other and with public health professionals. There are indeed many instances of such collaborations and initiatives across multiple platforms. Even when they are not the main participants, faith-based actors guide nongovernmental organizations, state authorities, and health practitioners in healthcare diplomacy. In the next section, I discuss the many ways interfaith communication happens on issues of health, including initiatives and conversations that took place during the current, most recent pandemic.

INTERFAITH INTERACTIONS FOR HEALTH AND HEALTHCARE

Interfaith dialogue on healthcare happens on many levels. It can either be situated in existing organizational frameworks or established in its own right to focus on a societal issue. Interfaith initiatives often happen with a common specific goal in mind; crises and public issues of importance can engender or consolidate interfaith relations and even lead to social transformation through these newfound connections.[18] I identify four levels—state, international, local, and religious organizational/individual—where interfaith interactions happen. As described below, many interfaith initiatives move across or operate at more than one level, so the levels should not be seen as mutually exclusive.

State Level: Interfaith interactions and diplomacy can happen with official governmental support. President Obama's Advisory Council on Faith-based and Neighborhood Partnerships, which was established in 2009 by an executive order, had a task force focusing on the role of faith-based and community organizations in global poverty, health, and development, which mostly focused on relief and humanitarian aid efforts. In Kenya, the government extended the mandate of the Interfaith Council—which is tasked with developing protocols for community gatherings such as religious worship, weddings, and funerals—to the end of 2021 "in recognition of the success recorded in the war against the COVID pandemic through the religious institutional structures."[19]

At the intersection of state and international levels, governments can also come together and establish platforms for interfaith initiatives. The King Abdullah bin Abdulaziz International Centre for Interreligious and Intercultural Dialogue (KAICIID) is a good example. It is an organization with leaders from Buddhist, Christian, Hindu, Jewish, and Muslim religious traditions, as well as the governments of Saudi Arabia, Austria, Spain, and the Holy See (as founding observer). Although there were criticisms of the organization due to Saudi Arabia's human rights record, the Centre has been welcomed by the United Nations.[20] The organization has various fellowship programs that are open to participants from around the world. These programs and the networks they establish sometimes lead to ground-up initiatives. For example, two of KAICIID's fellows, Sohini Jana from India and Jon Rasmussen from Denmark, created a Zoom-based support group that brought young people together with religious leaders and experts from various traditions around the world to share "faith-based best practices for supporting mental health, helping participants to find hope during COVID and understand the role of faith identities during intercommunity interactions around the virus."[21]

Interfaith dialogue also happens as part of larger agendas and contexts and not just as exclusively dialogues focused on religion. For example, interfaith conversations and religious outreach were only a part of a wider Swedish public health aspirational agenda, in addition to including other community leaders and representatives of various associations, especially those who are influential in marginalized communities.[22]

International Level: International organizations host, organize, and support interfaith initiatives, usually to take advantage of the access faith-based actors have in their capacity as leaders in communities of practice. The HIV/AIDS, Ebola, and COVID crises, especially, brought the influence of religious actors and interfaith diplomacy to the World Health Organization's attention.[23] WHO Director-General Tedros Adhanom Ghebreyesus emphasized the role of multi-faith/interfaith efforts to address vaccine inequity across the world.[24] UNICEF has also worked with local religious leaders and organized interfaith initiatives on child health and children's rights domains in settings ranging from Cambodia to Egypt.[25] A two-year-long collaboration between UNICEF and Muslim and Christian leaders in Sierra Leone increased immunization coverage of children under 1 year of age from 6% to 75%.[26] Similarly, the International Committee of the Red Cross supported an interfaith dialogue on the dignified management of the dead in India that was organized by Rajiv Gandhi National University of Law, Punjab in collaboration with the Indian chapter of the Temple of Understanding Foundation.[27]

With some interfaith experience under its belt before COVID, UNICEF was quick to launch interfaith initiatives when the pandemic started. In cooperation with Religions for Peace, it launched the "Global Multi-Religious Faith-in-Action COVID Initiative." In addition to senior leaders of various faith traditions, the initiative includes interfaith networks of youth and women. This is particularly important as women tend not to feature as prominently in interfaith initiatives (or major faith-based initiatives of any sort). The initiative included specific action items such as "the promotion of heightened focus on hygiene and sanitation in keeping with religious teachings and sacred texts that emphasize cleanliness as an element of holiness" and "countering all forms of stigma and discrimination associated with transmission of the disease with active promotion of attitudes and behaviors to uphold the dignity and rights of all people."[28] In April 2020, UNICEF's Regional Office for South Asia brought together thirty prominent religious and faith leaders from across South Asia in an online forum to brainstorm on how to protect vulnerable communities from COVID.[29]

After the pandemic started, various faith leaders discussed critical issues among themselves and brought key recommendations to intergovernmental forums like the G20. They addressed challenges related to the COVID in addition to education, structural inequality, and racism, all of which are directly related to access to healthcare. As part of this G20 interfaith forum, Christina Tobias-Nahi, the director of communications and public affairs at Islamic Relief USA, pointed to the centrality of interfaith diplomacy in tackling vaccine hesitancy and access: "There are many faith communities that will be reticent about the vaccination when it comes out for different religious reasons. If everyone needs to come together as humanity to tackle this mass health problem together, we're going to have to figure out a way to work together across faith communities and within faith communities to do this messaging."[30] Figuring out how to get healthcare messages and advisories out in a convincing manner is one of the functions of religious epistemic communities in healthcare.

Local Level: Faith leaders can come together under non-governmental organizations. The Interfaith Health Program (IHP), for example, was established in 1992 under the auspices of the Carter Center and currently operates out of the Rollins School of Public Health at Emory University. The initial focus of the program was on bringing together the Muslim, Christian, and Jewish communities of Atlanta, but later expanded to include international work primarily aimed at fighting HIV/AIDS. IHP contributed to teaching and research on interfaith communications about health, and thus had direct epistemic impact. Beginning in 1996, IHP established the Faith and Health Consortium, a network of interdisciplinary academic partners in various domestic and international locations that brought health sciences schools together with religious leaders and departments of religious studies to conduct research and instruction in addition to advancing community partnerships.[31]

Another city-level initiative, All Faiths Vaccination Campaign (described as "a partnership of over 60 entities and organizations from diverse faith traditions, health care institutions as well as government and civic leaders" on its website) aimed to promote the vaccine in Philadelphia. In addition to religious messaging aimed at informing black and brown communities about the vaccine, the campaign provided "at least 30 dedicated sites across various churches, mosques, and medical organizations in the city where residents can get their vaccines by appointment or walk-in."[32] In examples like this, one can clearly see that religious leaders do not only act as epistemic communities, but also as larger communities of practice that provide resources and enable access.

Religious Leadership/Organizational Level: Interfaith initiatives and involvement of religious leaders in healthcare can happen at the religious organizational and individual level without any government, international organization, or city administration involvement. The critical role religious actors played in response to the Ebola pandemic in West Africa constituted a learning experience for public health practitioners.[33]

In Sierra Leone, when international and local health organizations could not deal with Ebola by themselves, Muslim and Christian leaders came together, used their epistemic credibility, and "identified passages in the Quran and the Bible to give a religious context to new burial practices, showing that they were acceptable according to their faiths." A United Nations staff number described the involvement of faith leaders as "a game changer."[34]

There are also instances of religious organizations reaching out to the other faith-based actors on their own. The World Council of Churches and the Pontifical Council for Interreligious Dialogue jointly issued a statement called "Serving a Wounded World in Interreligious Solidarity: A Christian Call to Reflection and Action During COVID and Beyond," which aimed to "encourage churches and Christian organizations to reflect on the importance of interreligious solidarity in a world wounded by the COVID pandemic."[35] In 1989, "The Church's Challenge in Health" convention brought together 300 religious leaders representing diverse communities with health professionals. The convention produced a paper that addressed "contemporary primary health care issues," "the role of faith community in health and healing," and "mobilizing the faith community to respond to health needs."[36] Similarly, the Islamic Society of North America lists several interfaith initiatives it has actively taken part in on its website, including Faithful Reform in Healthcare and Faith United Against Tobacco. Christian and Muslim religious leaders in Malawi engaged in AIDS-related activities including "formal messages (i.e., preaching), pragmatic interventions (monitoring the sexual behavior of members and advising divorce to avoid infection), and the promotion of biomedical prevention strategies (promoting condom use and testing for HIV."[37] Religious actors can also use symbols and rituals to inspire their communities and organize interfaith prayer events that bring people together to affirm their commonality. An example of such an event is the Menifee Interfaith and Community Service Council's National Day of Prayer which brought religious leaders from diverse traditions together to lead prayers.[38]

FUTURE OF INTERFAITH INTERACTIONS ON HEALTH AND HEALTHCARE: LIMITATIONS AND POSSIBILITIES

There are many interfaith initiatives—at the individual, local, governmental, and international levels—that have advanced healthcare goals for their communities and played a key role in overcoming health challenges including the recent pandemic. These religious communications and projects are necessary as the healthcare systems in the United States and across the world are still facing many challenges in meeting the needs of communities. In this section, I note five important questions, contributions, and challenges of interfaith dialogue and diplomacy, each of which constitutes a research agenda for further exploration: (1) interfaith dialogue countering exclusionary religious interpretations in health while facing its own dynamics of inclusion and diversity, (2) religious positions and their fluidity, (3) questions on the nature of religious expertise and lay expertise, (4) the role of interfaith conversations in helping depoliticize healthcare conversations and underlining inclusion and cooperation, and (5) interfaith communications providing comfort and spiritual support through rituals and symbols.

To start with, interfaith communications have their own challenges of inclusion and diversity. Young representatives and women are often missing or excluded from interfaith initiatives.[39] Having said that, interfaith initiatives and diplomacy usually constitute necessary epistemic counterweights to religious interpretations that are not inclusive and peaceful. Interfaith communications and communities can address strict and exclusionary dynamics that involve one or more religions.[40] In a 2020 interfaith report penned by Mohammed Elsanousi, executive director of the Network for Religious and Traditional Peacemakers; Burton Visotzky, director of the Milstein Center for Interreligious Dialogue; and Bob Roberts, founding and senior pastor at Northwood Church, the authors recognize that "religious leaders and actors fail to adhere to the calls and continue to engage communities in religious gatherings" and "quite often, religious texts have been misinterpreted to justify patriarchy and gender-based inequalities."[41] They call on young people of faith "to supply their digital know-how to build good communication during the crisis" and encourage more discussions on "how the three religions can collaborate on charitable initiatives."[42]

In the framework of COVID, not all religious actors have been receptive to health experts' messaging. While many places of worship suspended services or moved to virtual or outdoor platforms,[43] others adamantly continued their in-person services in defiance of health advisories and represented COVID precautions as infringements on religious liberties.[44] Interfaith initiatives become even more critical for moderation in times of crises. There are myriad examples of religious extremism—including Islamophobia and antisemitism[45]—increasing during health crises as well as the cases of various religious actors—from diverse religious traditions in settings ranging from Israel to Russia—going against government measures by keeping places of worship open and organizing gatherings that turned out to be super-spreader events.[46] In some cases, religious actors might be co-opted by authoritarian state actors, as we saw in the case of Hungary's Orbán-led government.[47] Religious actors of different traditions and cultures coming together can help balance against these exclusionary epistemic dynamics, underline the importance of communications and partnership, and make it easier to communicate inclusive messages on issues ranging from sustainable economic practices to equitable healthcare policies. While reaching out to other traditions for inclusive messages, it is inevitable that religious actors will draw the ire of ultraconservatives in their own tradition. Pope Francis, for example, upon joining an interfaith day of prayer against COVID in 2020, was accused of cooperating with the "infidels" by some segments of the Catholic clergy.[48]

Second, interfaith communications and diplomacy on healthcare—or on any issue in general—becomes complicated when one acknowledges that there is no single definitive religious position on a given issue. There are multiple public theologies on any given issue in a faith tradition—contingent on time, space and different perspectives on spirituality—some of which might directly contradict others.[49] In 2016, for example, Pope Francis permitted the use of artificial contraceptives for women who are exposed to Zika, a departure from the Church's long-held blanket ban on contraceptives.[50] Religious interpretations can be fluid, which can be regarded as both positive and challenging. It is positive, because it means that even strict approaches can be modified to adapt to the circumstances. It can be challenging because these changes can undermine trust in religious institutions and texts and bring into question how legitimate a religion's position is if it can change at any moment.

Third, studying religious actors—as part of interfaith initiatives and diplomacy—as independent epistemic communities raises questions about the nature of expertise. How much should religious actors comment on health questions? Can they independently provide advice to their communities? In any case, to what extent do the communities look to religious leaders in the era of Google and Facebook? One of the challenges for interfaith or religious expertise is the democratization of knowledge. For many years now, there has been a shift from hierarchical orders and religious institutions (such as churches, synagogues, mosques) to multi-lingual webpages that facilitate self-interpretations of what is acceptable according to the text and what is not.[51] In the field of health, Akrich shows how online groups that share "lay expertise" and create "lay knowledge" can constitute their own epistemic communities that deconstruct professionals' positions.[52] Lay knowledge refers to "knowledge stemming from [personal] experience" and lay expertise "depicts the result of the appropriation of scientific knowledge by laypeople."[53] Religious actors might participate in the deconstruction of scientific expertise by resisting precautions laid out by the scientific community.

The changing nature of expertise and media have implications for the epistemic power of religious actors themselves. Specialized knowledge is not enough for religious legitimacy; "communicative character of religious authority" and being culturally relevant in the virtual/internet world is also critical.[54] This will become even more of an issue as we move out of the pandemic, a time when the internet featured even more prevalently in the lives of everyday people. In times of social isolation, experts and community leaders found new ways of reaching out to communities. The Spiritual Hotline Project implemented by Brazilian healthcare workers provided religious insights and spiritual comfort to people from various backgrounds.[55] The increasing centrality of social media during the pandemic also opened venues for interfaith initiatives. Religions for Peace, for example, organized an interfaith meeting on Facebook that brought together leaders from various traditions including the Muslim Grand Mufti of Uganda, a Nigerian Catholic Archbishop, and the Baha'i representative to the UN.[56]

Fourth, interfaith communications can help tackle healthcare challenges that are easily politicized. Religious traditions coming together can accentuate the parameters of human dignity and healthcare in a way that challenges political exploitation of a healthcare need. Yetunde, for example, points to the importance of Christian-Buddhist interreligious dialogue in the spiritual care of transgender hospital patients in the face of adverse political conditions and decreased resources.[57] There are also areas of healthcare where more interfaith initiatives are needed, given the diverse populations involved. For example, scholars have called for more interreligious dialogue and involvement to combat neglected tropical diseases that disproportionately affect Muslim, Hindu, and Catholic populations.[58]

Fifth, although this article mostly looked at interfaith dialogue that aims to bolster implementation and increase the reach of healthcare initiatives, such partnerships can also contribute rituals and symbols of spiritual meaning and strength. Prayer has been an important spiritual resource that has long been neglected by community projects and initiatives.[59] With COVID, interfaith prayers continued to be symbolically important. Jerusalem's religious leaders from the Christian, Jewish, Muslim, Druze, and Bahai traditions occasionally prayed together for the end of the virus.[60] Similar events and gatherings—in-person and virtual—took place around the world to show support for patients and healthcare workers, and to commemorate those who have passed away from the illness.[61]

CONCLUSION

Religious actors have networks and legitimacy among their communities that allows them to share messages and implement policies. This article argued that in addition to being communities of practice, they constitute epistemic communities characterized by a shared understanding of humanity, its relationship with the divine, and the expertise that come with it. In healthcare—as well as in other realms of policy—interfaith dialogue and diplomacy constitute special epistemic acts in countering exclusivist interpretations of faith by emphasizing common values, sharing messages, and helping implement policies. Religious interpretations and perspectives have the power to shape what is acceptable in the policy world, so their contributions to healthcare discussions are critical. In most, if not all, cases, interfaith interactions render these contributions more inclusive by nature of reaching out to and thinking with the "other."

The article enumerated the multiple ways interfaith interactions happen in healthcare. Religious leaders and organizations come together—sometimes with health experts and other policymakers—at the individual, regional, national, and international levels. Sometimes they happen within the framework of existing interfaith platforms with state and organizational support; other times, they develop in response to the crises of the time. Future investigations will need to compare the effectiveness of these multiple platforms and support structures.

To conclude, interfaith dialogues and diplomacy remain necessary in a politically divided world. Although this article looks at how religious actors worked together in healthcare, it is not just the religious leaders who can and should conduct interfaith initiatives and develop these necessary skills. Healthcare providers should also acquire interfaith literacy and have conversations with their patients in order to better serve communities with different perspectives, constraints, and prescriptions when it comes to medical interventions.[62] Community leaders, and anyone who has an interest in implementing inclusive policies, would benefit from familiarizing themselves with the precepts of other religions and coming together with members of different faith traditions.

NOTES

1. Liebermann and Schwartz, "Muslim and Jewish Paramedics Pause to Pray Together."
2. Sloan, Bagiella, and Powell, "Religion, Spirituality, and Medicine"; Koenig, King, and Carson, *Handbook of Religion and Health*; Lüddeckens, Hetmanczyk, Klassen, and Stein, *Routledge Handbook of Religion, Medicine, and Health*.
3. Haas, "Banning Chlorofluorocarbons," 3.
4. Adler, "The Spread of Security Communities," 199.
5. Adler, "The Spread of Security Communities," 200; Cross, *The European Diplomatic Corps*.
6. Sandal, *Religious Leaders and Conflict Transformation*.
7. Hall, Koenig, and Meador, "Conceptualizing Religion," 388.
8. Sandal, "Religious Actors as Epistemic Communities," 934.
9. Jotkowitz, Agbaria, and Glick, "Medical Ethics in Israel," 2584.
10. Jerving, "Why Liberians Thought Ebola Was a Government Scam."
11. Jacobs, "Conspiracy Theories About Zika Spread."
12. Barthe and Gilbert, "Impuretés et Compromis de l'expertise."
13. Cohen-Fournier, Brass, and Kirmayer, "Decolonizing Health Care."
14. Payne, "Ottawa Public Health Turns to Faith Leaders."
15. "Faith leaders sign common declaration ahead of COP26."
16. "Educate," CHIP Community Health Interfaith Partnership, http://www.chipgeorgia.com/educate.html.
17. Bravante and Ong, "Interfaith Dialogue."
18. Widianto, Perguna, Thoriquttyas, and Hasanah, "Reorganizing the Ummah."
19. Kihiu, "Kenya: Government Extends Mandate."
20. Ki-moon, "Untitled."
21. "Virtual Interfaith Dialogue Platform Provides Youth with Mental Health Support During COVID-19," KAICIID, January 28, 2021, https://www.kaiciid.org/news-events/features/virtual-interfaith-dialogue-platform-provides-youth-mental-health-support.
22. Valeriani et al., "Addressing Healthcare Gaps in Sweden during the COVID-19 Outbreak."
23. Winiger and Peng-Keller, "Religion and the World Health Organization."

24. Tedros, "Untitled."
25. Hanmer, "Child Rights Organizations and Religious Communities."
26. Zarocostas, "UNICEF Taps Religious Leaders in Vaccination Push," 1709.
27. International Committee of the Red Cross, "India: Interfaith Dialogue."
28. "Launch of Global Multi-Religious Faith-in-Action Covid-19 Initiative," UNICEF, April 7, 2020, https://www.unicef.org/press-releases/launch-global-multi-religious-faith-action-covid-19-initiative.
29. "Religious and Faith Leaders Join Hands to Protect Women and Children," UNICEF, May 19, 2020, https://www.unicef.org/rosa/stories/religious-and-faith-leaders-join-hands-protect-women-and-children.
30. Welsh, "Faith Leaders Bring Recommendations to G-20."
31. "History and Milestones," Interfaith Health Program, https://ihpemory.org/ihp-what-we-do/history-and-milestones/.
32. Ahébée, "Philadelphia's Faith Leaders."
33. Marshall, "Roles of Religious Actors in the West African Ebola Response."
34. "Keeping the Faith: The Role of Faith Leaders in the Ebola Response," ReliefWeb, July 30, 2015, https://reliefweb.int/report/sierra-leone/keeping-faith-role-faith-leaders-ebola-response.
35. World Council of Churches, "Serving a Wounded World in Interreligious Solidarity."
36. International Health Program, *The Church's Challenge in Health*.
37. Trintapoli, "The AIDS-related Activities of Religious Leaders in Malawi."
38. "Interfaith Council to Host National Day of Prayer," Menifee 24/7, April 30, 2021, https://www.menifee247.com/2021/04/interfaith-council-to-host-national-day-of-prayer-event.html.
39. Weller, "How Participation Changes Things."
40. Clark, "Local Groups Offer Advice for Getting Involved in Interfaith Efforts."
41. Elsanousi, Visotzky, and Roberts, "Love your Neighbour."
42. Elsanousi, et al., "Love your Neighbour."
43. Sulkowski and Ignatowski, "Impact of COVID-19 Pandemic."
44. Haynes, "Donald Trump, the Christian Right and COVID-19"; Conger, Healy, and Tompkins, "Churches Were Eager to Reopen."
45. Morthorst, "Scapegoating of Religious Minorities During Covid-19"; Fishman, "As Coronavirus Cases Spike in Turkey, So Does anti-Semitism."
46. Yendell, Hidalgo, and Hillenbrand, *The Role of Religious Actors in the COVID-19 Pandemic*.
47. Hidalgo, "Religious Backgrounds of Illiberal Democracy in Eastern Europe."
48. Pullella, "Pope Joins Inter-faith Prayers Against Coronavirus."
49. Sandal, "The Clash of Public Theologies?"
50. Romero and Yardley, "Francis Says Contraception Can Be Used to Slow Zika."
51. Cheong, Poon, Huang, and Casas, "The Internet Highway and Religious Communities."
52. Akrich, "From Communities of Practice to Epistemic Communities," 117.

53   Akrich, "From Communities of Practice to Epistemic Communities," 117.
54   Cheong, Huang, and Poon, "Religious Communication and Epistemic Authority," 948.
55   Ribeiro et al., "The Role of Spirituality in the COVID-19 Pandemic."
56   Judd, "Inspiring Interfaith Moments."
57   Yetunde, *Buddhist-Christian Dialogue.*
58   Hotez and Aksoy, "An Interfaith Dialogue"; Hotez, "The World's Great Religions."
59   Schwarz, "Challenging the Ontological Boundaries."
60   Judd, "Inspiring Interfaith Moments."
61   Patterson and Lowe, "Interfaith Day of Mourning"; Judin, "Faith Leaders Mourn"; Asala, "Interfaith Prayer Groups Show Solidarity."
62   Bellwood, "Doctors and Diversity."

REFERENCES

Adler, Emanuel. "The Spread of Security Communities: Communities of Practice, Self-restraint, and NATO's Post—Cold War Transformation." *European Journal of International Relations* 14, no. 2 (2008): 195–230. https://doi.org/10.1177/1354066108089241.

Ahébée, Sojourner. "Philadelphia's Faith Leaders Partner with One Another and the City to Increase Vaccine Access in Communities of Color," WHYY, June 12, 2021. https://whyy.org/articles/philadelphias-faith-leaders-partner-with-one-another-and-the-city-to-increase-vaccine-access-in-communities-of-color/.

Akrich, Madeleine. "From Communities of Practice to Epistemic Communities: Health Mobilizations on the Internet." *Sociological Research Online* 15, no. 2 (2010): 116–32. https://doi.org/10.5153/sro.2152.

Asala, Kizzi. "Interfaith Prayer Groups Show Solidarity Outside Cape Town Hospitals," Africanews, January 21, 2021. https://www.africanews.com/2021/01/21/interfaith-prayer-groups-show-solidarity-outside-cape-town-hospitals/.

Barthe, Yannick, and Claude Gilbert. "Impuretés et Compromis de l'expertise, une Difficile Reconnaissance : À Propos des Risques Collectifs et des Situations d'incertitude." In *Le Recours aux Experts : Raisons et Usages Politiques*, edited by Laurence Dumoulin, Stéphane La Branche, Cécile Robert, and Philippe Warin, 43–62. Grenoble: Grenoble University Press, 2005.

Bellwood, Leslie. "Doctors and Diversity: Using Interfaith Literacy and Interfaith Dialogue to Improve Patient Care." *Dialog* 58, no. 3 (2019): 217–24. https://doi.org/10.1111/dial.12486.

Bravante, Meriam A., and Rubirose R. Ong, "Interfaith Dialogue: Mental Wellness and Healthy Relationship." Action Dignity, January 18, 2020. https://actiondignity.org/wpcontent/uploads/2021/02/Session-Notes-ActionDignity-Interfaith-Dialogue-January-18-2020.pdf

Cheong, Pauline Hope, Jessie P.H. Poon, Shirlena Huang, and Irene Casas. "The Internet Highway and Religious Communities: Mapping and Contesting

Spaces in Religion-Online." *The Information Society* 25, no. 5 (2009): 291–302. https://doi.org/10.1080/01972240903212466.

Cheong, Pauline Hope, Shirlena Huang, and Jessie P.H. Poon. "Religious Communication and Epistemic Authority of Leaders in Wired Faith Organizations." *Journal of Communication* 61, no. 5 (2011): 938–58. https://doi.org/10.1111/j.14602466.2011.01579.x.

Clark, Charles T. "Local Groups Offer Advice for Getting Involved in Interfaith Efforts," *San Diego Union Tribune*, August 27, 2021. https://www.sandiegouniontribune.com/columnists/story/2021-08-27/column-interfaith-groups-efforts-to-promote-religious-tolerance.

Cohen-Fournier, Sara Marie, Gregory Brass, and Laurence J. Kirmayer. "Decolonizing Health Care: Challenges of Cultural and Epistemic Pluralism in Medical Decision-making with Indigenous Communities." *Bioethics* 35, no. 8 (2021): 767–78. https://doi.org/10.1111/bioe.12946.

Conger, Kate, Jack Healy, and Lucy Tompkins. "Churches Were Eager to Reopen. Now They Are Confronting Coronavirus Cases," *New York Times,* July 8, 2020. https://www.nytimes.com/2020/07/08/us/coronavirus-churches-outbreaks.html.

Cross, Mai'a K. Davis. *The European Diplomatic Corps: Diplomats and International Cooperation from Westphalia to Maastricht.* New York: Palgrave Macmillan, 2007.

CHIP Community Health Interfaith Partnership. "Educate." Accessed August 26, 2022. http://www.chipgeorgia.com/educate.html.

Elsanousi, Mohamed, Burton L. Visotzky, and Bob Roberts. "Love your Neighbour: Islam, Judaism and Christianity Come Together over COVID-19," World Economic Forum, April 9, 2020. https://www.weforum.org/agenda/2020/04/religions-covid-19-coronavirus-collaboration/.

Fishman, Louis. "As Coronavirus Cases Spike in Turkey, So Does anti-Semitism," *Haaretz*, March 19, 2020. https://www.haaretz.com/middle-east-news/turkey/.premium-as-coronavirus-cases-spike-in-turkey-so-does-anti-semitism-1.8682725.

Haas, Peter M. "Banning Chlorofluorocarbons: Epistemic Community Efforts to Protect Stratospheric Ozone." *International Organization* 46, no. 1 (1992): 187–224. https://doi.org/10.1017/S002081830000148X.

Hall, Daniel E., Harold George Koenig, and Keith G. Meador. "Conceptualizing 'Religion': How Language Shapes and Constrains Knowledge in the Study of Religion and Health." *Perspectives in Biology and Medicine* 47, no. 3 (2004): 386–401. https://doi.org/10.1353/pbm.2004.0050.

Hanmer, Stephen. "Child Rights Organizations and Religious Communities: Powerful Partnerships for Children." *CrossCurrents* 60, no. 3 (September 2010): 451–61. https://doi.org/10.1111/j.1939-3881.2010.00142.x.

Haynes, Jeffrey. "Donald Trump, the Christian Right and COVID-19: The Politics of Religious Freedom." *Laws* 10, no. 1 (2021): 11–27. https://doi.org/10.3390/laws10010006.

Hidalgo, Oliver. "Religious Backgrounds of Illiberal Democracy in Eastern Europe." *Journal of Religion and Society in Central and Eastern Europe* 12, no. 1 (December 2019): 3–21. https://rascee.net/index.php/rascee/article/view/104.

Interfaith Health Program. "History and Milestones." Accessed August 26, 2022. https://ihpemory.org/ihp-what-we-do/history-and-milestones/.

Hotez, Peter J., and Serap Aksoy. "An Interfaith Dialogue on the Neglected Tropical Diseases." *PLOS Neglected Tropical Diseases* 5, no. 12 (2011): e1240. https://doi.org/10.1371/journal.pntd.0001240.

Hotez, Peter J. "The World's Great Religions and their Neglected Tropical Diseases." *PLOS Neglected Tropical Diseases* 10, no. 7 (2016): e0004544. https://doi.org/10.1371/journal.pntd.0004544.

Independent Catholic News. "Faith leaders sign common declaration ahead of COP26." September 22, 2021. https://www.indcatholicnews.com/news/43093.

International Committee of the Red Cross. "India: Interfaith Dialogue on Dignified Management of the Dead during COVID-19," August 12, 2020. https://www.icrc.org/en/document/india-interfaith-dialogue-dignified-management-dead-during-covid-19.

Menifee 24/7. "Interfaith Council to Host National Day of Prayer," April 30, 2021. https://www.menifee247.com/2021/04/interfaith-council-to-host-national-day-of-prayer-event.html.

International Health Program. *The Church's Challenge in Health.* Occasional Paper Series 1, no. 2. Atlanta: Carter Center of Emory University, 1989. https://ihpemory.org/wp-content/uploads/2014/08/The%20Churchs%20Challenge%20in%20Health.pdf.

Jacobs, Andrew. "Conspiracy Theories About Zika Spread Through Brazil With the Virus," *New York Times*, February 16, 2016. https://www.nytimes.com/2016/02/17/world/americas/conspiracy-theories-about-zika-spread-along-with-the-virus.html.

Jerving, Sara. "Why Liberians Thought Ebola Was a Government Scam to Attract Western Aid," *The Nation*, September 16, 2014. https://www.thenation.com/article/archive/why-liberians-thought-ebola-was-government-scam-attract-western-aid/.

Jotkowitz, Alan B., Riad Agbaria, and Shimon M. Glick. "Medical Ethics in Israel—Bridging Religious and Secular Values." *The Lancet* 389, no.10088 (2017): 2584–86. https://doi.org/10.1016/S0140-6736(17)30700-6.

Judd, Emily. "Inspiring Interfaith Moments during the Coronavirus Pandemic," *Alarabiya News,* April 2, 2020. https://english.alarabiya.net/features/2020/04/02/Inspiring-interfaith-moments-during-the-coronavirus-pandemic.

Judin, Nick. "Faith Leaders Mourn, Memorialize 10,000 Mississippians Lost to Coronavirus," *Mississippi Free Press*, November 4, 2021. https://www.mississippifreepress.org/17865/faith-leaders-mourn-memorialize-10000-mississippians-lost-to-covid-19/.

ReliefWeb. "Keeping the Faith: The Role of Faith Leaders in the Ebola Response," July 30, 2015. https://reliefweb.int/report/sierra-leone/keeping-faith-role-faith-leaders-ebola-response.

Ki-moon, Ban. "Untitled." Transcript of Secretary-General Ban Ki-moon's remarks at Inauguration Ceremony of the King Abdullah bin Abdulaziz International Centre for Interreligious and Intercultural Dialogue, Lisbon, November 26, 2012. https://www.un.org/sg/en/content/sg/statement/2012-11-26/secretary-general-ban-ki-moons-remarks-inauguration-ceremony-king.

Kihiu, Njoki. "Kenya: Government Extends Mandate of Interfaith Council to Dec 31 Over Covid-19 Spike," AllAfrica, June 21, 2021. https://allafrica.com/stories/202106220139.html.

Koenig, Harold, Dana King, and Verna B. Carson. *Handbook of Religion and Health*. New York: Oxford University Press, 2012.

UNICEF. "Launch of Global Multi-Religious Faith-in-Action Covid-19 Initiative," April 7, 2020. https://www.unicef.org/press-releases/launch-global-multi-religious-faith-action-covid-19-initiative.

Liebermann, Oren, and Michael Schwartz. "Muslim and Jewish Paramedics Pause to Pray Together," CNN, March 26, 2020. https://www.cnn.com/2020/03/26/middleeast/israel-muslim-jew-coronavirus-paramedic-intl/index.html.

Lüddeckens, Dorothea, Philipp Hetmanczyk, Pamela E. Klassen, and Justin B. Stein. *The Routledge Handbook of Religion, Medicine and Health*. New York: Routledge, 2021.

Marshall, Katherine. "Roles of Religious Actors in the West African Ebola Response." *Development in Practice* 27, no. 5 (2017): 622–33. https://doi.org/10.1080/09614524.2017.1327573.

Morthorst, Lasse. "Scapegoating of Religious Minorities During Covid-19: Is History Repeating Itself?," Institute of Development Studies, June 29, 2020. https://www.ids.ac.uk/opinions/scapegoating-of-religious-minorities-during-covid-19-is-history-repeating-itself/

Patterson, Jerrita, and Zaneta Lowe. "Interfaith Day of Mourning to be held at Crosstown Concourse," WREG Memphis, November 2, 2021. https://www.wreg.com/news/local/interfaith-day-of-mourning-to-be-held-at-crosstown-concourse/.

Payne, Elizabeth. "Ottawa Public Health Turns to Faith Leaders for Help with Mental Health Crisis," *Ottawa Citizen*, September 17, 2021. https://ottawacitizen.com/news/local-news/ottawa-public-health-turns-to-faith-leaders-for-help-with-mental-health-crisis.

Pullella, Philip. "Pope Joins Interfaith Prayers Against Coronavirus, Irks Ultraconservatives," Reuters, May 14, 2020. https://www.reuters.com/article/us-health-coronavirus-pope-prayer-idUSKBN22Q2KJ.

Ramsey-Lucas, Curtis. "Faith and Mental Health: Creating a Culture of Encounter and Friendship." *Review & Expositor* 113, no. 2 (2016): 198–204. https://doi.org/10.1177/0034637316639006.

UNICEF. "Religious and Faith Leaders Join Hands to Protect Women and Children," May 19, 2020. https://www.unicef.org/rosa/stories/religious-and-faith-leaders-join-hands-protect-women-and-children.

Ribeiro, Marcus Renato Castro, Rodolfo Furlan Damiano, Ricardo Marujo, Fabio Nasri, and Giancarlo Lucchetti. "The Role of Spirituality in the COVID-19 Pandemic: A Spiritual Hotline Project." *Journal of Public Health* 42, no. 4 (December 2020): 855–56. https://doi.org/10.1093/pubmed/fdaa120.

Romero, Simon, and Jim Yardley. "Francis Says Contraception Can Be Used to Slow Zika," *New York Times*, 18 February 2016. https://www.nytimes.com/2016/02/19/world/americas/francis-says-contraception-can-be-used-to-slow-zika.html.

Sandal, Nukhet A. "Religious Actors as Epistemic Communities in Conflict Transformation: The Cases of South Africa and Northern Ireland." *Review of International Studies* 37, no. 3 (2011): 929–49. https://doi.org/10.1017/S0260210510001592.

———. "The Clash of Public Theologies? Rethinking the Concept of Religion in Global Politics." *Alternatives* 37, no. 1 (2012): 66–83. https://doi.org/10.1177/0304375412439675.

———. *Religious Leaders and Conflict Transformation: Northern Ireland and Beyond.* New York: Cambridge University Press, 2017.

Schwarz, Tanya B. "Challenging the Ontological Boundaries of Religious Practices in International Relations Scholarship," *International Studies Review* 20, no. 1 (2018): 30–54. https://doi.org/10.1093/isr/vix030.

World Council of Churches. "Serving a Wounded World in Interreligious Solidarity: A Christian Call to Reflection and Action During COVID-19 and Beyond," August 27, 2020. https://www.oikoumene.org/resources/documents/serving-a-wounded-world-in-interreligious-solidarity-a-christian-call-to-reflection-and-action-during-covid-19-and-beyond.

Sloan, Richard P., Emilia Bagiella, and Tia Powell. "Religion, Spirituality, and Medicine." *The Lancet* 353, no. 9153 (1999): 664–67. https://doi.org/10.1016/S0140-6736(98)07376-0.

Sulkowski, Lukasz, and Grzegorz Ignatowski. "Impact of COVID-19 Pandemic on Organization of Religious Behaviour in Different Christian Denominations in Poland." *Religions* 11, no. 5 (2020): 254–69. https://doi.org/10.3390/rel11050254.

Tedros Adhanom Ghebreyesus. "Untitled." Transcript of WHO Director-General's opening remarks at high-level dialogue on multi-religious response to COVID-19 vaccine, March 19, 2021. https://www.who.int/director-general/speeches/detail/who-director-general-s-opening-remarks-at-high-level-dialogue-on-multi-religious-response-to-covid-19-vaccine.

Trintapoli, Jenny. "The AIDS-related Activities of Religious Leaders in Malawi." *Global Public Health* 6, no. 1 (2011): 41–55. https://doi.org/10.1080/17441692.2010.486764.

Valeriani, Giuseppe, Iris Sarajlic Vukovic, Tomas Lindegaard, Roberto Felizia, Richard Mollica, and Gerhard Andersson. "Addressing Healthcare Gaps in Sweden during the COVID-19 Outbreak: On Community Outreach and Empowering Ethnic Minority Groups in a Digitalized Context." *Healthcare* 8, no.4 (2020): 445–54. https://doi.org/10.3390/healthcare8040445.

KAICIID. "Virtual Interfaith Dialogue Platform Provides Youth with Mental Health Support During COVID-19," January 28, 2021. https://www.kaiciid.org/news-events/features/virtual-interfaith-dialogue-platform-provides-youth-mental-health-support.

Yendell, Alexander, Oliver Hidalgo, and Carolin Hillenbrand. *The Role of Religious Actors in the COVID-19 Pandemic: A Theory-based Empirical Analysis with Policy Recommendations for Action*. Stuttgart: Institut für Auslandsbeziehungen, 2021.

Welsh, Teresa. "Faith Leaders Bring Recommendations to G-20," Devex, November 19, 2020. https://www.devex.com/news/faith-leaders-bring-recommendations-to-g-20-98592.

Widianto, Ahmad Arif, Luhung Perguna, Titis Thoriquttyas, and Fitriatul Hasanah. "Reorganizing the Ummah: COVID-19 and Social Transformation in Plural Society." In *Community Empowerment through Research, Innovation and Open Access: Proceedings of the 3rd International Conference on Humanities and Social Sciences (ICHSS 2020), Malang, Indonesia, 28 October 2020*, 151–55. Abingdon, UK: Routledge, 2021.

Weller, Paul. "How Participation Changes Things: 'Inter-Faith', 'Multi-Faith' and a New Public Imaginary." In *Faith in the Public Realm: Controversies, Policies and Practices*, edited by Adam Dinham, Robert Furbey, and Vivien Lowndes, 63–81. Bristol: Policy Press, 2009.

Winiger, Fabian, and Simon Peng-Keller. "Religion and the World Health Organization: An Evolving Relationship." *BMJ Global Health* 6, no. 4 (2021): e004073. https://doi.org/10.1136/bmjgh-2020-004073.

Yetunde, Pamela Ayo. *Buddhist-Christian Dialogue, US Law, and Womanist Theology for Transgender Spiritual Care*. London: Springer, 2020.

Zarocostas, John. "UNICEF Taps Religious Leaders in Vaccination Push." *The Lancet* 363, no. 9422 (2004): 1709–11. https://doi.org/10.1016/S0140-6736(04)16294-6.

JUYAN ZHANG

PUTTING INTERFAITH DIALOGUE ON THE PUBLIC DIPLOMACY RADAR
Goals, Power, Strategies, and the Influence of Worldviews

INTRODUCTION

Since the 1893 World's Parliament of Religions, interfaith dialogue has gained traction in world affairs. It has become a domestic concern for countries with different religious faiths and the need to promote interfaith understanding and harmonious coexistence.[1] It has become a diplomatic instrument as states increasingly realize the role of religion in shaping international relations.[2] The beginning of the twenty-first century saw even more interest in interfaith dialogue. Rapid growth of communication technology and increased international migration have brought people of different religions into closer contact.[3] States have tapped religion as a source of soft power, and religious organizations have actively expanded their influence in the world arena. At the same time, religious hostilities are on the rise.[4]

Research has shown that interfaith dialogue can contribute to personal, relational, and structural changes.[5] On the micro level, members of interfaith groups experience relational, personal, and transformative learning.[6] On the macro level, interfaith dialogue brings about positive changes to global affairs. For example, after the Second Vatican Council made positive statements about other religions and recognized the unity of humankind,[7] the Roman Catholic Church redefined its position by focusing on religious freedom, poverty, engagement with various cultures, and nuclear disarmament.[8]

Against such a backdrop, nation states have shown increasing interest in using interfaith dialogue for diplomacy. In the post-September 11 world, policymakers have recognized that religion continues to be a strong source of personal motivation and that foreign policy and security analysis need to incorporate an understanding of religion.[9] Accordingly, faith-based diplomacy has been recognized as an essential area of expertise.[10]

CONGRUENCE BETWEEN PUBLIC DIPLOMACY AND INTERFAITH DIALOGUE

Interfaith dialogue at the international level shares significant similarities with public diplomacy. Public diplomacy is defined as a relationship management function that promotes strategic people-to-people communication to establish a sustaining relationship.[11] Similarly, interfaith dialogue is "an intentional encounter between individuals who adhere to differing religious beliefs and practices in an effort to foster respect and cooperation among these groups through organized dialogue."[12] Public diplomacy is regarded as a dialogical form of international political communication aimed at creating mutually beneficial relations.[13] Similarly, interfaith dialogue is regarded as one of the most important political instruments for reaching across borders and building bridges of peace and hope.[14]

There is also significant congruence between public diplomacy and interfaith dialogue in terms of the changes they bring about. Neufeldt observed three approaches regarding how change occurs through interfaith dialogue. The theological approach aims at understanding each other's doctrines, worldviews, and personal experiences. The political approach aims at generating social coexistence and legitimizing or delegitimizing a political process or actor. The peacebuilding approach aims at developing a joint platform for conflict resolution.[15] Among the three approaches, the theological approach matches cultural diplomacy, which refers to long-term public diplomacy that promotes understanding of a nation's culture; the political approach matches engagement diplomacy, which aims at creating shared resources and fashioning a common language;[16] and the peacebuilding approach matches conflict resolution in public diplomacy. Such congruence makes it possible to examine how interfaith dialogue fits into public diplomacy.

DIALOGUE AS TWO-WAY SYMMETRICAL COMMUNICATION

Interfaith dialogue is often portrayed as an effort to foster respect, cooperation, tolerance, and collaboration. Real-world dialogue, however, is a more complicated process. An organization may engage in sham dialogue and have no intention of conceding,[17] while well-intentioned dialogue may generate no results. James E. Grunig's excellence theory, the most influential theory in the field of public relations, can greatly inform our understanding of the dynamics of interfaith dialogue. The theory's notion of two-way symmetrical communication has been equated with dialogue.[18] In the two-way symmetrical model, organizations use communication to adjust their ideas and behavior to those of others. Grunig argues that the model represents the most ethical and effective public relations. Critics argue that the model is unrealistic because organizations hire public relations people not as "do-gooders" but as advocates for their interests.[19] Priscilla Murphy combines game theory and the two-way symmetrical model to construct the mixed-motive model of public relations, which suggests that it is possible to be cooperative and competitive in the same campaign.[20] In the model, the organization and public can both retain a strong sense of self-interest, yet each is motivated to cooperate in a limited fashion to resolve any conflict.[21] Grunig agrees that the mixed-motive model best represents two-way communication, and it can only be realized if its primary motivation is to find the win-win strategy.[22] He argues that asymmetrical tactics may be used to gain the best position for organizations within the win-win zone.[23] Kenneth Plowman identifies nine approaches an organization may take in a mixed-motive situation. Among them, contention, avoidance, and principled approaches are closer to the one-way extreme in which organizations win and the public loses. Accommodation, compromise, and mediated communication fall at the other end of the continuum where the interests of the public become more important than the organization's interests. In the middle, or the win-win zone, are cooperation, unconditionally constructive, and win-win or no deal tactics. Numerous quantitative studies have corroborated excellence theory. Rhetorical studies have also substantiated it. Grunig notes that advancements based on Burke and Habermas's theories counterbalance the sender orientation of traditional rhetoric with an emphasis on receiver orientation.[24]

The mixed-motive model informs interfaith dialogue in the following aspects. First, commensurate with the overarching tenets of dialogism, the model points to the win-win zone as the ideal goal of two-way communication.[25] Second, dialogue does not always imply collaboration or result in win-win outcomes. Instead, in a dialogue, all nine strategies Plowman identifies may be present. Third, genuine two-way communication is based on the symmetrical worldview because genuine dialogue is based on ethics.[26] Finally, dialogue involves not only rational arguments but also rhetoric and narratives.

MAPPING THE USE OF INTERFAITH DIALOGUE IN PUBLIC DIPLOMACY: THE INTERFAITH DIALOGUE-PUBLIC DIPLOMACY (ID-PD) RADAR

In this essay, I adapted the public diplomacy radar that I developed in an earlier publication to map the use of interfaith dialogue in public diplomacy. The adapted framework is labeled the ID-PD Radar (Figure 1). The main framework of the ID-PD Radar consists of two perpendicular axes representing ethics and efficacy. The ethics spectrum ranges from compassion to manipulation, respectively represented by the Buddha and Niccolò Machiavelli. A compassionate stance seeks to foster positive emotions in order to enhance the overall standing of a PD actor. A manipulative stance is much more direct in that it seeks to lead others to adopt concrete actions or policy changes. The efficacy spectrum ranges from narrative to rational argument, respectively represented by Walter Fisher and Edward Burke at one end, and Plato and Socrates at the other. The intersection of these two axes marks the center of a "dish" of five concentric circles. Starting at the center, the circles represent A) goals, B) power, C) worldviews, D) public diplomacy practices that interfaith dialogue may contribute to,[27] and E) likely interfaith dialogue strategies.

ETHICS AND EFFICACY

Ethics
Ethics is one of the most important concerns for public relations and public diplomacy.[28] For interfaith dialogue, ethics is essential not only because it is the basis of any type of dialogue[29] but also because religion and ethics are inextricably and genetically intertwined—ethics is the soil in which religion grows.[30] Religion advocates for compassion. At the same time, the history of religion is associated with manipulation, conflict, and killings. As such, ethics in interfaith dialogue is a spectrum that ranges between manipulation and compassion (the horizontal axis in the ID-PD Radar). When interfaith dialogue is involved in public diplomacy, the issue of ethics becomes complicated. Religious organizations need to not only determine their moral stances on the dialogical subjects but also face ethical questions that arise from their involvement in diplomacy.

Consider the dispute that occurred during the World Fellowship of Buddhists (WFB) conference in Seoul, South Korea, in 2012. The Chinese delegation boycotted the conference's opening ceremony after its demand

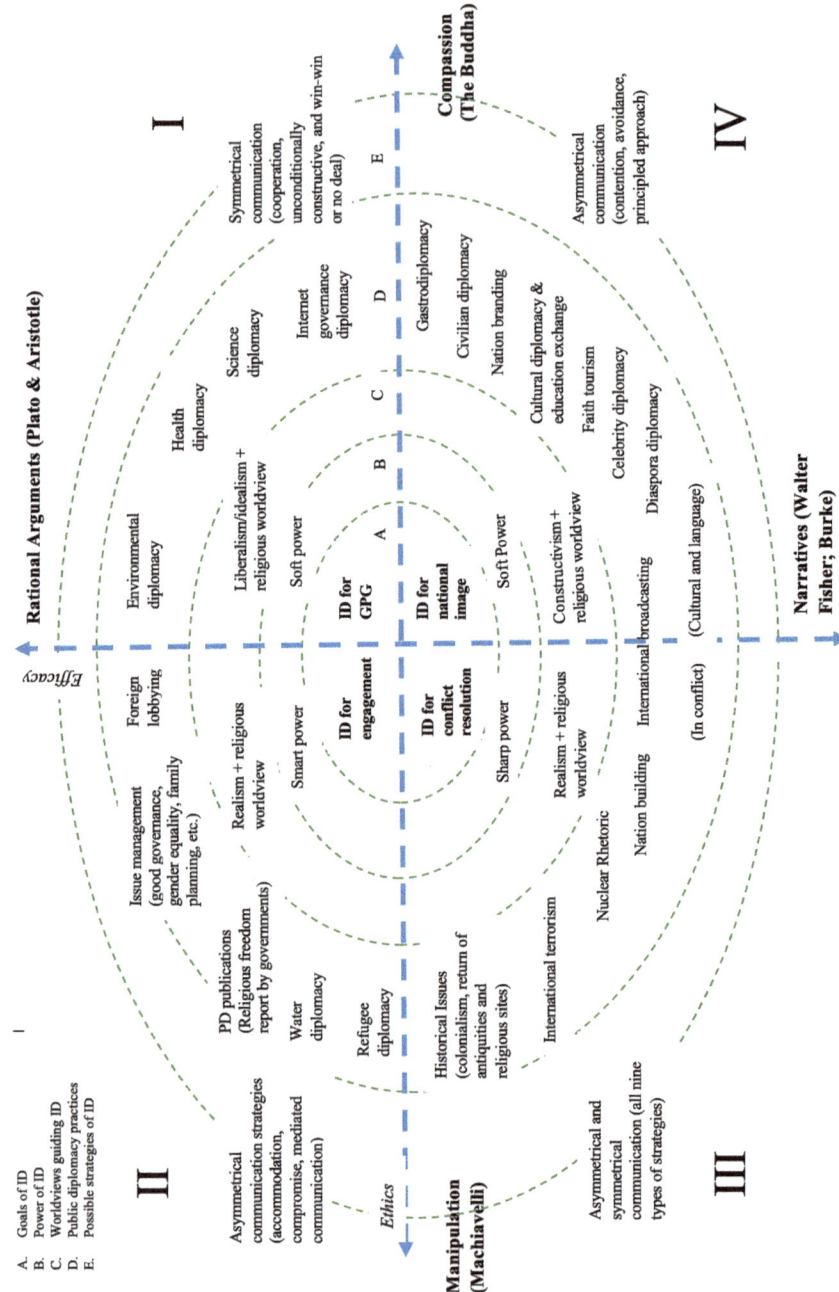

Figure 1. The ID-PD Radar

that Buddhist representatives from the Tibetan government-in-exile leave the conference was rejected. It then abruptly withdrew from the conference. The South Korean organizer, the Jogye Order, stated that the Chinese delegation's action "goes against the universal value of solidarity and the promotion of peace" and noted that the Tibetan affiliates were officially registered with the WFB. It requested a formal apology from the Chinese delegation.[31] In this case, the delegations from different Buddhist traditions were undoubtedly engaged in public diplomacy. South Korea used the conference as an opportunity to globalize Korean Buddhism.[32] The Chinese government controls and directs China's delegation. Meanwhile, promoting Tibetan Buddhism is the most important means for the Tibetan government-in-exile to demonstrate its existence. In the dispute, the Chinese delegation's actions undercut its moral ground, whereas the South Korean delegation's actions reinforced its moral ground by adhering to the "value of solidarity and the promotion of peace."

Efficacy

Efficacy is the communication paradigm that ranges between the rational argument paradigm and the narrative paradigm. The former argues that humans make decisions based on logic and arguments. The latter suggests that people make decisions based on good reasons.[33] Religion has a deeply narrative structure, and narrative provides the substance of faith.[34] In interfaith dialogue, religious organizations need to not only share their narratives but also use rational arguments (the vertical axis in the ID-PD Radar).

Consider the interfaith dialogue on climate change, an urgent problem that requires interreligious effort to solve.[35] Different religions have different narratives regarding the relationship between humans and the planet. Regarding the ecological crisis, however, science and its evidence-based argumentation provide the arena for a new kind of interreligious dialogue.[36] At the Interfaith Summit on Climate Change, held in New York in 2014, religious leaders presented an interfaith statement on climate change to the United Nations and called on world leaders to work constructively toward a global climate agreement. Thus, the interfaith dialogue was a public diplomacy event. In their statement, the religious leaders used the rational argument paradigm to make their case. They declared, "We acknowledge the overwhelming scientific evidence that climate change is human-induced and . . . we are ready to dialogue with those who remain skeptical."[37]

GOALS OF INTERFAITH DIALOGUE IN PUBLIC DIPLOMACY

Interfaith dialogue may contribute to four types of public diplomacy goals. These include global public goods (GPG), national image, engagement diplomacy, and conflict resolution. Goals are fundamental in the ID-PD Radar because they may condition the nature of power, PD practices that interfaith dialogue contributes to, and the strategies a party adopts.

Interfaith dialogue for GPGs
GPGs refer to the common goods of humankind. They are a way of understanding trans-border and global problems and the need for a coordinated international response.[38] Interfaith dialogue will not only promote the quality of religion as a public good;[39] it can also contribute to other types of GPGs by facilitating global cooperation, creating and building agendas, promoting mutual understanding, and involving nongovernmental actors and international organizations.[40] In recent years, religious communities have engaged in dialogues and taken actions to address issues that pose challenges to GPGs. The International Partnership on Religion and Sustainable Development, an interfaith dialogue project launched in 2016, connects government bodies, faith-based organizations, and civil society agencies in order to encourage communication on religion and sustainable development.[41] Water and Faith, an interfaith dialogue event organized by the Stockholm International Water Institute, stated that "stories from our different traditions and the ethical understanding of water as a common good play a central role in protecting and influencing the way we value and use water."[42] In general, to achieve such goals, goodwill, candidness, and rational arguments are necessary (Sphere I in the ID-PD Radar).

Interfaith dialogue for engagement and policy agendas
Interfaith dialogue may contribute to engagement diplomacy in non-conflict situations to achieve specific policy agendas. Engagement diplomacy aims to "inject new thinking and ideas; create shared resources; promote dialogue; [and] fashion a common language."[43] In interfaith dialogue for engagement, rational arguments and cost-effective calculations are needed (Sphere II in the ID-PD Radar). The Obama

administration incorporated interfaith dialogue into its signature engagement diplomacy. In January 2010, the U.S. Department of State convened a U.S.-Indonesia Interfaith Conference in Jakarta. Faith leaders from various countries, along with leaders from the private sector and civil society, shared best practices to enhance collaboration in areas such as poverty alleviation, education, and environmental protection.[44] In March 2010, the United States Agency for International Development (USAID) hosted a regional conference on the "role of religious leaders in advancing development in Asia" in Dhaka, Bangladesh.[45] Religious and community leaders from across Asia shared ideas on the roles that traditional leaders of society play in promoting good governance, gender equality, health, and family planning, among other areas.[46] USAID defined its strategic religious engagement as "the process of collaborating with religious communities and/or partnering with faith-based organizations to advance shared development goals."[47] In 2013, the U.S. government adopted the U.S. National Strategy on Religious Leader and Faith Community Engagement, which encourages American diplomats and development professionals to engage with religious leaders and faith communities. The U.S. government has since included religious actors in its civil society engagement around the world, a priority again underscored in the 2020 Presidential Executive Order on Advancing International Religious Freedom by the White House.[48] The Obama administration set up the Office of Faith-Based and Neighborhood Partnerships to handle interreligious cooperation. It worked with the National Security Council, Department of State, USAID, and Corporation for National and Community Service to foster dialogue and cooperation at home and around the globe.[49]

China has tapped interfaith dialogue as an engagement instrument in its Belt and Road Initiative (BRI), which is a key component of the Chinese Communist Party's diplomatic policy. When the Boao Forum for Asia, an international organization of twenty-nine member states that aims to "promote economic integration in Asia,"[50] held its 2021 annual conference, it included an interfaith dialogue seminar. The China Religious Culture Communication Association (CRCCA) and China Committee on Religion and Peace (CCRP), two semi-official organizations tasked with public diplomacy, hosted the seminar. The theme of the seminar, "Inclusiveness, mutual learning, collaboration among ten-thousands of states: The wisdom and mission of religion in the Belt and Route," shows that the seminar is an engagement instrument for China to promote the BRI.[51]

Interfaith dialogue as engagement diplomacy may occur between theocracies. Since 1994, the Iranian government and the Vatican have held interfaith dialogue through Iran's Center for Interfaith Dialogue and the Vatican's Pontifical Council for Interreligious Dialogue. Muslim and Christian scholars and academics participated in the panels and discussed issues such as rights and duties of a person, family, education of the youth, and service to society.[52]

In recent years, interfaith dialogue for engagement and policy agendas has gone beyond concerns of national interest and become a pan-global initiative seeking solutions to global issues. The G20 Interfaith Forum, inaugurated in 2014, has become an annual platform where religious networks engage in global agendas in the host country of the G20, an intergovernmental forum comprising twenty of the largest economies in the world. The forum describes its goal as being "to contribute meaningful insight and recommendations that respond to and help shape the G20 and thus global policy agendas."[53] It has considered wide-ranging agendas, including economic models and systems, the environment, women, families, children, work, humanitarian aid, health, education, freedom of religion or belief, global security, governance, human rights, and the rule of law.[54]

Interfaith dialogue for conflict resolution
Interfaith dialogue may become a public diplomacy channel for conflict resolution.[55] The assumption of its use in such a context is that conflicts are in part due to misunderstandings, and interfaith dialogue may help reduce and eliminate misunderstandings. Interfaith dialogue first became a global concern after the September 11 terrorist attacks. In 2004, the UN General Assembly passed a resolution on "the promotion of interfaith dialogue." The next year, interfaith dialogue was institutionalized as a UN function. The United Nations Alliance of Civilizations was created and placed under the direct leadership of the UN Secretary-General,[56] who sponsored meetings to promote interreligious and intercultural understanding.[57] The Bush administration also enlisted interfaith dialogue for its anti-terrorism war. For example, in 2006, Karen Hughes, who was then undersecretary of state for public diplomacy and public affairs, made it clear that interfaith dialogue is vital to combat terrorist ideologies.[58]

Ironically, in some cases, efforts to promote interfaith dialogue may lead to conflict. Austrian politicians criticized the King Abdullah bin Abdulaziz International Centre for Interreligious and Intercultural

Dialogue (KAICIID), which if funded by Saudi Arabia and headquartered in Vienna, because of Saudi Arabia's history of human rights violations. News media reported that the center would be relocated as a result of the conflict.[59] When an interfaith dialogue project sponsored by the German government called "the House of One" included the Gülen movement, which Turkey labelled a terrorist organization, Turkey called on Germany to "return from this grave mistake" and requested that "the true representatives of the Muslims" be included in the project.[60]

Theocracies caught in conflict may engage in interfaith dialogue. For example, the Germany-based Center for Applied Research in Partnership with the Orient (CARPO) has established an Iran-Saudi dialogue initiative to facilitate the exchange of opinions on issues that concern the two countries.[61] Additionally, interfaith dialogue is used when nations dispute over historical religious sites. When the Turkish government revoked the museum status of the Hagia Sophia and gave it to the Muslim community for public worship in 2020, the Holy Synod of the Russian Orthodox Church called for "further promotion and strengthening of mutual respect and understanding between believers of various world religions."[62] In interfaith dialogue conflict resolution, narrative and manipulation are more likely used (Sphere III in the ID-PD Radar).

Interfaith dialogue for cultivating a national image
Interfaith dialogue may be used to cultivate a country's image, which is the main goal of public diplomacy. First, secular states may enlist interfaith dialogue to promote their images. In 2020, China's CCRP held a virtual international conference, where China's religious leaders shared with their international counterparts "the experience of inter-religious collaboration in combating the coronavirus pandemic."[63] The event occurred at a time when dispute arose surrounding the origin of the virus and China's national image was tarnished. In preparation for the World Conference for Interreligious and Intercultural Dialogue in Moscow, Russia invited Miguel Angel Moratinos, the UN Undersecretary-General, to visit the country. The leader of Russia's Interreligious Council promoted the Russian image by telling the UN official that "people of various traditional religions and cultures have peacefully co-existed in Russia for many centuries and accumulated a great experience of interreligious dialogue and cooperation."[64]

Theocracies and countries whose governance is conditioned by religion may use interfaith dialogue to cultivate their images as well. In

2008, Saudi Arabia invited religious scholars, media, and academics from around the world for interfaith talks. Saudi Crown Prince Mohammed bin Salman said that he wanted to return Saudi Arabia to a "moderate Islam" that is more open to the world and tolerant of other faiths.[65] Qatar has been branding itself a hub of interfaith dialogue by sponsoring the Doha International Centre for Interfaith Dialogue and the U.S.-Islamic World Forum.[66] The United Arab Emirates has arranged mutual visits between Pope Francis and the Grand Imam of al-Azhar, Dr. Ahmad al-Tayeb, as part of the country's nation branding campaign.[67] During the 1990s, Turkey's state institution, the Directorate of Religious Affairs (Diyanet), pursued interreligious dialogue with the Christian Church in Europe when developing relations with the European Union became Turkey's national priority.[68] Indonesia, home to the world's largest Muslim population, conducted interfaith dialogue with the United States after the September 11 terrorist attacks to improve the image of Islam.[69]

In some cases, successful domestic interfaith dialogue may contribute to a country's image. Singapore is one of the most religiously diverse countries in the world, but in more than half a century, there has not been a single religious conflict there.[70] Religious harmony has contributed to the country's image as a global business hub. Overall, to cultivate a nation's image, goodwill and appealing narratives are desirable, but manipulation is possible (Sphere IV in the ID-PD Radar).

WORLDVIEW CONDITIONING ON INTERFAITH DIALOGUE IN PUBLIC DIPLOMACY

Worldviews that states hold, including stances on international relations, state-religion dynamics, and theological positions, may condition interfaith dialogue in public diplomacy. Theories of realism, idealism, liberalism, and constructivism, either individually or together, may explain or influence worldviews on international relations. Realism suggests that the international system is anarchic, and states always seek to maximize their power and self-interest.[71] Interfaith dialogue, if used for public diplomacy within such a worldview, may serve mainly as an instrument for image cultivation (Sphere IV in the ID-PD Radar but significantly weighs toward manipulation) and engagement (Sphere II). Russia, for example, has long regarded interfaith dialogue as a central component of its international image and an asset of state diplomacy.[72] The Chinese state directs China's international interfaith dialogue and the semi-official CCRP conducts it. The latter's stated mission is to "further exchanges and cooperation with the religious circles in all countries" and "safeguard the unification of the motherland."[73] Interfaith dialogue guided by realism may lack autonomy and genuineness. It may use both rational arguments and narratives, but in general, it uses manipulation instead of demonstrating compassion.

In contrast, idealism holds that international relations should be based on morality, international law, and international institutions;[74] liberalism suggests that international organizations and NGOs may play important roles in shaping state behavior;[75] and constructivism argues that identity, ideas, perceptions, and their social constructions are important to determine actors' behavior.[76] For states that harbor such worldviews, genuine interfaith dialogue is more likely to occur, and grassroots-level interfaith dialogue organized by NGOs is encouraged. The Joint Learning Initiative on Faith and Local Communities, a U.S.-based organization, states that its mission is "full and appropriate engagement of the capacities of faith actors in the achievement of humanitarian and development goals through effective partnerships with public sector and secular entities, as well as among religious groups themselves."[77] It seeks solutions for issues such as human trafficking and modern slavery and aims to end violence against children and refugees. Interfaith dialogue based on such worldviews may use both rational arguments and narratives and harbor compassion. (Sphere I of the ID-PD Radar).

Worldviews on state-religion relations may condition interfaith dialogue in public diplomacy. The separation of church and state in secular states may limit the role of the government in interfaith dialogue. The U.S. government established the first White House Office of Faith-Based and Community Initiatives during President George W. Bush's administration. President Bush declared that the efforts of religious and other community organizations cannot replace government, but government can and should welcome such organizations as partners.[78] Treating faith communities as partners may allow more autonomy for these communities to engage in genuine interfaith dialogue. In countries such as China, Vietnam, and Cuba, the communist ideology that regards religion as the opium of the masses may condition interfaith dialogue for realpolitik purposes. Cuba, for example, held an "International Meeting for Inter-religious Dialogue and the World Peace" in 2015. In addition to pledging to work for a better world, the participants called on the United States to end its sanctions against Cuba, defended the independence cause of Puerto Rico, and demanded the return of the Malvinas Islands to Argentina.[79]

For states where theological worldviews dominate or significantly shape polity, use of interfaith dialogue in public diplomacy may become complicated because of dual conditioning by state and religion. On the one hand, these countries may use interfaith dialogue as a state apparatus based on a rational calculation of national interest. On the other hand, these regimes' theological views may limit the scope and depth of dialogue. In June 2008, Saudi Arabia held an interfaith dialogue in Mecca. Saudi King Abdullah and Iranian politician Akbar Hashemi Rafsanjani sat side by side to deliver a message of reconciliation between Shiite and Sunni Muslims.[80] However, geopolitical conflict between the two countries and the theological schism between the two regimes rendered dialogue fruitless, as the continued proxy conflicts in Yemen and Syria in the past decade demonstrated. Turkey's diplomacy had long been conducted with a realism-based worldview; in the 1990s, it even entertained ideas of liberalism by reducing state control of religion.[81] As the country's governance has become increasingly Islamized since 2013, however, Turkey's relationships with other countries have likewise become more complicated.

INTERFAITH DIALOGUE AND POWER

Interfaith dialogue may add to three types of power when it is enlisted for public diplomacy: soft power, smart power, and sharp power. Soft power refers to a country's attractiveness based on its culture, political values, and foreign policies.[82] Interfaith dialogue may add to soft power by contributing to GPG and cultivating a country's image. The Indian government has actively tapped Buddhism as a resource of soft power.[83] In 2011, with its assistance, about 900 high-ranking Buddhist monks from different Buddhist traditions attended the Global Buddhist Congregation in India, leading to the formation of the International Buddhist Confederation.[84] In November 2021, the Indian Council for Cultural Relations, a government organization that conducts cultural diplomacy, launched "the first edition of the Global Buddhist Conference."[85] The goal is determining "how to make India the center of Buddhism."[86] Russia has used interfaith dialogue to promote its international image as a unique civilization in which different religions harmoniously coexist, thus boosting its soft power.[87] When interfaith dialogue is enlisted for soft power, both narrative and rational persuasion may be used, but invariably this requires ethics. A lack of ethics will not make a country attractive (Spheres I and IV of the ID-PD Radar).

Interfaith dialogue may contribute to a country's smart power, which is a combination of soft power and hard power.[88] Smart power is commensurate with the concept of engagement diplomacy—that is, diplomacy along with sanctions and military force.[89] The Obama administration fully embraced the doctrine of smart power,[90] and it enlisted interfaith dialogue in its diplomacy. When Muslim countries sought a UN resolution to condemn defamation of religion and legitimize Islamic laws penalizing perceived religious blasphemy, the United States brokered an agreement that removed defamatory language and instead focused on eliminating religious discrimination. Hillary Clinton's speech at an interfaith conference in Turkey summarized such "smartness" in power brokerage. She stated that she was hopeful a religious tolerance agreement between the West and Islamic countries would end efforts to criminalize blasphemy that threatened freedom of expression.[91] The background of the U.S.'s interfaith dialogue with the Islamic world included 2011's "Arab Spring" and the anti-terrorism campaigns of the 2000s and 2010s, which required the full spectrum of the U.S.'s hard power and soft power. When interfaith dialogue is used for smart power, rational arguments along with different degrees of manipulation are necessary (Sphere II of the ID-PD Radar).

Last, interfaith dialogue may contribute to a country's "sharp power," a recent concept that refers to aggressive public diplomacy campaigns by authoritarian countries including Russia, China, Saudi Arabia, and Turkey.[92] The United Arab Emirates has used interfaith dialogue for nation branding, but the country has also engaged in military interventions in Yemen and Libya. Interfaith dialogue thus becomes a tool of "sharp power."[93] Saudi Arabia has advocated for interfaith dialogue, but the country's conflict with Iran and the assassination of the dissident journalist Jamal Khashoggi in 2018 have made its rhetoric unconvincing. When interfaith dialogue becomes a tool of sharp power, manipulation and narratives are used (Sphere III of the ID-PD Radar).

PUBLIC DIPLOMACY PRACTICES AND INTERFAITH DIALOGUE STRATEGIES

As the mixed-motive model of excellence theory demonstrates, organizations may use asymmetrical and symmetrical strategies at the same time to communicate with their public. In interfaith dialogue, the party's goals, worldviews, and power, along with the public diplomacy practices of interfaith dialogue, may shape the strategies it adopts.

Interfaith dialogue may contribute to GPG-oriented public diplomacy practices, such as environmental diplomacy, science diplomacy, and Internet governance diplomacy (Circle D in Sphere I). Because of GPG's nonrivalrous and nonexclusive nature,[94] parties in interfaith dialogue about such practices are less likely to become competitive, and their dialogic strategies are most likely to fall within the win-win zone (cooperation, unconditionally constructive, and win-win or no deal tactics) (Sphere I).

Interfaith dialogue may contribute to national image-oriented public diplomacy practices, such as gastrodiplomacy (e.g., promotion of religious foods and rituals), civilian diplomacy, nation branding, cultural and education diplomacy, faith tourism, celebrity diplomacy (e.g., visits by major religious figures), international broadcasting, and diaspora diplomacy (Circle D in Sphere IV). When interfaith dialogue is used for cultivating a national image, dialogue strategies are more likely to be at the asymmetrical extremes of advocacy (contention, avoidance, and principled approaches) (Sphere IV). The fact that national image needs cultivation, repair, and defense conditions this notion. The U.S.'s promotion of interfaith dialogue in the Middle East was partly intended to repair its image, which was tarnished by its invasion of Iraq. At an interfaith conference held in Turkey in July 2011, U.S. Secretary of State Hillary Clinton used a principled approach and stated that an initiative by the United States, the European Union, and the Organization of the Islamic Conference would promote religious freedom without compromising free speech.[95] Taking a principled approach, Turkey's Diyanet stated that interfaith dialogue "should not be understood as assimilation; rather every religion stays within its borders, keeps its distinctive features, does not attempt any compulsion, should talk on common issues of tolerance and understanding, and should look for collaboration."[96] For China, international interfaith dialogue mainly serves as an instrument to cultivate its national image. When Chinese delegates withdrew from the Buddhist conference in Seoul, South Korea in 2012, China used contention and avoidance. In 2017, China used again avoidance by choosing not to send a delegation to the International Buddhist Conference because the Dalai Lama had been invited to inaugurate the conference.[97]

Interfaith dialogue may be involved in engagement diplomacy practices such as lobbying (e.g., Vatican's lobbying in the United States), issue management (e.g., USAID-sponsored activities), public diplomacy-oriented publications (e.g., the U.S. Government's annual report on world religious freedom), water diplomacy, and refugee diplomacy (Circle D in Sphere II). When interfaith dialogue is used for engagement, asymmetrical communication of accommodation (accommodation, compromise, and mediated communication) may be used (Sphere II). This is conditioned by the nature of engagement diplomacy, which aims to create shared resources and fashion a common language. Dialogue subjects may include security, freedom of speech, religious freedom, gender equality, and so on. During the 2020 Evidence Summit on Strategic Religious Engagement that USAID hosted, nearly 300 individuals from around the world presented their research on the impact of collaborating with religious communities and partnering with faith-based organizations.[98] Such collaboration and partnership must involve accommodation, compromise, and mediated communication, whereas contention and avoidance should be avoided.

Lastly, when interfaith dialogue is used for conflict resolution in public diplomacy, the whole range of symmetrical and asymmetrical dialogue strategies may be used (Sphere III). Subjects of interfaith dialogue may include disputes over historical issues (e.g., the legacy of colonialism or repatriation of religious artifacts), international terrorism, nuclear issues, nation building after conflicts, and international broadcasting surrounding conflicts (Circle D in Sphere III). Turkey's decision to turn the Hagia Sophia into a mosque illustrates that all nine types of dialogue strategy may be used in a conflict situation. Because the case involves almost every aspect of interfaith dialogue and public diplomacy, I will use it to not only demonstrate possible dialogue strategies in a conflict situation but also illustrate the various aspects of interfaith dialogue in public diplomacy.

CASE STUDY: INTERFAITH DIALOGUE AS PUBLIC DIPLOMACY IN THE HAGIA SOPHIA CONTROVERSY

The Hagia Sophia was built in the sixth century as a Byzantine church. After the Ottoman conquest of Istanbul in 1453, it was turned into a mosque. In 1934, the Hagia Sophia was converted into a museum as a part of Turkey's secularization efforts. Later, it became a UNESCO World Heritage Site. Since the mid-2000s, the Turkish government has enlisted interfaith dialogue for its global soft power campaign. It has built two thousand Ottoman-style mosques in the world, many of which the Diyanet controls.[99] In July 2020, Turkey's highest administrative court revoked the Hagia Sophia's museum status. Turkey's president, Recep Tayyip Erdoğan, issued a decree that turned it into a mosque.

Turkey's policies, actions, and rhetoric surrounding the Hagia Sophia are undoubtedly related to public diplomacy, and so is the international community's response. Every dimension of public diplomacy-oriented interfaith dialogue can be found in the case of the Hagia Sophia.

Ethics and efficacy
In terms of ethics, Shared Sacred Sites, a global campaign that promotes interfaith dialogue, has issued a compassionate call to turn Hagia Sophia back into a shared sacred site.[100] President Erdoğan's initial decree was a manipulative act, as designating the site a mosque would bring it under Diyanet's control, regardless of the fact that the decree would violate international law.[101] In terms of efficacy, UNESCO made a rational argument by noting that the site was officially included on the World Heritage List as a museum, entailing legal commitments and obligations.[102] The Turkish government responded with the narrative that the functional usage of the Hagia Sophia is "solely related to Turkey's sovereign rights."[103] During the dispute, President Erdoğan tweeted a video of the Hagia Sophia, calling it "a symbol of the re-rising of the sun of our civilization."[104]

Goals of interfaith dialogue
All four types of goals of interfaith dialogue in public diplomacy are manifested in the Hagia Sophia case. First, the Hagia Sophia is a GPG, and dialogue surrounding the site is related to faith and public diplomacy. As UNESCO noted, the Hagia Sophia's status "as a museum reflects the universal nature of its heritage, and makes it a powerful symbol for dialogue."[105] Second, the site is essential for Turkey's national image, and Turkey's move caused damage to this image. Third, Turkey's decision caused a conflict that involved many parties: Turkish Islamists who wished to pray at the site, Christians who regarded the building as a church, secularists who see the site as a cultural landmark, and UNESCO who regards it as a world heritage site. Last, Turkey's decision is a part of its engagement diplomacy, which not only includes building mosques around the world but also providing aid operations through the Turkish Cooperation and Coordination Agency.[106]

Worldviews and power
The conditioning by worldviews of interfaith dialogue is explicit in the Hagia Sophia case. Since the 1980s, with a realism-centered worldview, Turkey has promoted a moderate form of nationalist Islam abroad to

combat leftist movements. In the 1990s, entertaining liberalism, Turkey used interreligious dialogue to advance its case for membership in the European Union. The policy continued in the early 2000s because it was useful for maintaining Turkey's relationship with the EU. The country's full embracing of soft power also shows the influence of constructivism. After 2011, however, as the Turkish government became increasingly authoritarian and anti-Western, interfaith dialogue used Islam as an ideological tool for social engineering.[107] Turkey's decision surrounding the Hagia Sophia represents the culmination of a shift in its worldview on international relations, which its theological worldview further compounded.

The power manifested in Turkey's public diplomacy evolved accordingly. Until 2013, Turkey was perceived positively as an actor in the arena of soft power and a budding democracy.[108] However, as the country became increasingly authoritarian, its soft power campaigns become perceived as a projection of "sharp power."[109] From Turkey's perspective, however, it had used "smart power," not sharp power.[110]

Strategies in interfaith dialogue
The various parties involved in the controversy adopted strategies ranging from asymmetrical communication to symmetrical communication. UNESCO adopted the principled approach by noting that Turkey's action violated international law. The Turkish government used contention to defend its move, and the Greek and Russian Orthodox churches condemned the move. When President Erdoğan talked to Russian President Vladimir Putin, he assured the latter that access to the site would be "guaranteed for all those who wish to visit, including foreign citizens, while the Christian relics will be preserved."[111] The rhetoric shows a certain degree of accommodation.

Shared Sacred Sites held an exhibition in Istanbul featuring the Hagia Sophia and the theme of tolerance and peaceful coexistence.[112] The World Council of Churches, the world's largest ecumenical organization representing over 500 million Christians, urged Turkey to reconsider its decision "in the interests of promoting mutual understanding, respect, dialogue and co-operation."[113] The strategies by both organizations fall into the realm of symmetrical communication (cooperation, unconditionally constructive, and win-win/no-deal).

In summary, the Hagia Sophia case represents a conflict situation where multiple parties engaged in interfaith dialogue. The outcome, in the short run, does not fall into the win-win zone. The backdrop of the conflict is Turkey's failed bid to become an EU member, partially as a result of the latter's perception of the incompatibility between Europe and Islam.[114] This perception, ironically, was why Turkey initiated interfaith dialogue back in the 1990s.

FINAL COMMENTS

As countries increasingly recognize the importance of interfaith dialogue and enlist it for public diplomacy, some issues that are related to it but have been underappreciated need more attention from academia, the religious community, and policymakers. First, religious organizations are morally obligated to engage in dialogue for a better world, and interfaith dialogue is not a favor or a discretion they can choose to adopt or ignore. Religious animosity has fueled many of the world's issues, such as the regional confrontation between the Shiite and Sunni countries and the conflict between Israel and Palestine. Historically, Christian actors have been closely associated with European powers' colonization of the world, and coloniality continues to impact today's world.[115] Second, when interfaith dialogue is used for cultivating a national image, religion becomes a state apparatus and genuine interfaith dialogue is less likely to take place. As such, separation of state and church should continue serving as a guiding principle when interfaith dialogue is enlisted for public diplomacy. Third, genuine interfaith dialogue is likely to occur on issues relating to GPG, engagement, and conflict resolution. The community-based interfaith dialogue programs developed by the Obama administration seem to be a functional model that other interfaith dialogue initiatives can adapt. Fourth, some successful domestic interfaith dialogue models may be expanded into bilateral and regional interfaith dialogue mechanisms, which may further develop into a global network of interfaith dialogue. Lastly, religious tourism, as one of the biggest segments of the tourist economy, may become a robust platform for interfaith dialogue at the grassroots level. Indonesia, for example, plans to promote the country's ancient Buddhist temple, Borobudur, as a global Buddhist tourism destination.[116] Pakistan has tapped the country's Buddhist and Jain ruins in ancient Gandhara as resources of faith tourism.[117] Both countries have emphasized the importance of multicultural coexistence and religious harmony in their initiatives.

NOTES

1 Agrawal and Barratt, "Does Proximity Matter in Promoting Interfaith Dialogue?," 568.
2 Hunter, "How Effective Is Interfaith Dialogue as an Instrument for Bridging International Differences and Achieving Conflict Resolution?," 102–3.
3 Keaten and Soukup, "Dialogue and Religious Otherness," 168.
4 "Religious Hostilities Reach Six-Year High" (Pew Research Center, January 14, 2014).
5 Neufeldt, "Interfaith Dialogue," 344.
6 Pope, "'This Is a Head, Hearts, and Hands Enterprise.'"
7 Fitzgerald, "Vatican II and Interfaith Dialogue," 4.
8 Chu, "Vatican Diplomacy in China and Vietnam," 58.
9 McDonagh et al., *On the Significance of Religion for Global Diplomacy*, 6.; Baker, "Religion and Diplomacy," 258.
10 Johnston, *Faith-Based Diplomacy*.
11 Payne, "Reflections on Public Diplomacy," 579.
12 Agrawal and Barratt, "Does Proximity Matter in Promoting Interfaith Dialogue?," 579. In the current research, "interfaith" refers to the relations between different religions and the relations between different traditions within a religion.
13 Ociepka, "Public Diplomacy as Political Communication," 291.
14 "General Assembly President Stresses Value of Interfaith Dialogue in Securing Peace," quoted in Neufeldt, "Interfaith Dialogue," 344–45.
15 Neufeldt, "Interfaith Dialogue," 349–54.
16 Evans and Steven, "Towards a Theory of Influence for Twenty-First Century Foreign Policy," 24.
17 Cancel, Mitrook, and Cameron, "Testing the Contingency Theory of Accommodation in Public Relations."
18 Theunissen and Wan Noordin, "Revisiting the Concept 'Dialogue' in Public Relations," 5.
19 Grunig and White, "The Effect of Worldviews on Public Relations Theory and Practice."
20 Murphy, "The Limits of Symmetry."
21 Grunig, "Two-way Symmetrical Public Relations."
22 Plowman, Briggs, and Huang, "Public Relations and Conflict Resolution."
23 Grunig, Grunig, and Dozier, *Excellent Public Relations and Effective Organizations*, 15.
24 Grunig and White, "The Effect of Worldviews," 48.
25 Kent and Taylor, "Toward a Dialogic Theory of Public Relations," 25–30.
26 Kent and Taylor, "Building Dialogic Relationships through the World Wide Web," 324.
27 The location of a PD practice in the radar is charted by asking two questions: On the ethics continuum, where is the PD practice most likely located? On the efficacy continuum, where is it most likely be located?

28 Grunig, "Two-Way Symmetrical Public Relations."
29 Kent and Taylor, "Building Dialogic Relationships," 324.
30 Knitter, "A Common Creation Story? Interreligious Dialogue and Ecology," 289.
31 "Buddhists Regret China's Boycott of World Conference," *Korea Times*, June 14, 2012.
32 Do, "Korea's Isolated Buddhism Opening Doors."
33 Griffin, Ledbetter, and Sparks, *A First Look at Communication Theory*, 300.
34 Burley, "Narrative Philosophy: Apologetic and Pluralistic Orientations," 5.
35 Knitter, "A Common Creation Story?" 289.
36 Knitter, "A Common Creation Story?" 286.
37 "Interfaith Statement on Climate Change," World Council of Churches, September 21, 2014.
38 Long and Woolley, "Global Public Goods: Critique of a UN Discourse."
39 Sherlock, "Religiosity as a Public Good," 3.
40 Zhang and Swartz. "Public Diplomacy to Promote Global Public Goods (GPG): Conceptual Expansion, Ethical Grounds, and Rhetoric."
41 Joint Learning Initiative on Faith & Local Communities, "International Partnership on Religion & Sustainable Development (PaRD)."
42 Stockholm International Water Institute, "Valuing Water - Interfaith Statement on Water and Faith from the SIWI Swedish Water House Cluster Group."
43 Evans and Steven, "Towards a Theory of Influence," 56.
44 U.S. Department of State, "Jakarta Interfaith Event."
45 U. S. Agency for International Development, "U.S. Sponsors Bangladesh Conference for Religious and Community Leaders on Advancing Development in Asia."
46 U. S. Agency for International Development, "U.S. Sponsors Bangladesh Conference."
47 USAID, "2020 Evidence Summit on Strategic Religious Engagement."
48 USAID, "2020 Evidence Summit."
49 Obama White House Archives, "Promoting Interfaith Dialogue and Cooperation."
50 Boao Forum for Asia, "About BFA."
51 Mao, "2021 Boao Forum for Asia Religious Sub-Forum Held"; translation by the author.
52 International Quran News Agency, "Iran, Vatican Inter-Religious Dialogue."
53 G20 Interfaith Forum, "About G20 Interfaith Forum."
54 G20 Interfaith Forum, "About G20 Interfaith Forum."
55 Hunter, "How Effective Is Interfaith Dialogue," 109, 111.
56 Haynes, "The United Nations Alliance of Civilizations and Interfaith Dialogue: What is it Good For?," 48–49.
57 General Assembly of the United Nations. "Culture of Peace: High-Level Dialogue on Interreligious and Intercultural Understanding and Cooperation for Peace."

58 Radio Free Europe/Radio Liberty, "U.S.: Undersecretary Of State Pushes For More Interfaith Dialogue."
59 Reuters, "Austria to Shut Saudi-backed Religious Dialogue Center."
60 Guler, "Turkey Slams FETO Terror Group-Backed Interfaith Dialogue Project in Germany."
61 Center for Applied Research in Partnership with the Orient, "Iran-Saudi Dialogue."
62 Russian Orthodox Church, "Statement of Russian Orthodox Church's Holy Synod Concerning Decision of Turkish Authorities to Change Status of Hagia Sophia."
63 China News Service. "Representatives of Religions and Peace Organizations from around the World Explore Interfaith Collaboration to Combat Coronavirus Pandemic."
64 Russian Orthodox Church, "Members of Interreligious Council in Russia Meet with Mr. Miguel Angel Moratinos, UN Under-Secretary-General, High Representative for Alliance of Civilizations."
65 Al-Kinnani, "Saudi Arabia Taking Lead in Interfaith Dialogue."
66 Fahy, "International Relations and Faith-Based Diplomacy: The Case of Qatar," 77.
67 Kourgiotis, "'Moderate Islam' Made in the United Arab Emirates: Public Diplomacy and the Politics of Containment," 7.
68 Yilmaz and Barry, "Instrumentalizing Islam in a 'Secular' State: Turkey's Diyanet and Interfaith Dialogue," 12.
69 Saragih, Surya, and Islamiah, "Indonesia's Effort to Improve Islamic Images in The United States During 2009–2017: A Case Study of Interfaith Dialogue."
70 Musa, "Inter-Faith Dialogue in Singapore Must Go Deeper."
71 Frieden and Lake, "Introduction."
72 Curanović, *The Religious Diplomacy of the Russian Federation*, 5–6.
73 China Committee on Religion and Peace, "China Committee on Religion and Peace."
74 Wilson, "Idealism in International Relations."
75 Doyle and Recchia, "Liberalism in International Relations."
76 Hopf, "The Promise of Constructivism in International Relations Theory," 181.
77 Joint Learning Initiative on Faith & Local Communities, "Mission & Vision."
78 The White House, "Fact Sheet: President Biden Reestablishes the White House Office of Faith-Based and Neighborhood Partnerships."
79 Martínez, "Inter-Religious Meeting for Dialogue and World Peace Wraps Up in Havana."
80 NBC News, "Saudi King Calls for End to Islamic Extremism."
81 Bertrand, "Turkish Diplomacy Since 2003: Transition from Realpolitik to a Liberal Foreign Policy?," 68.
82 Nye, "Hard, Soft, and Smart Power," 567.
83 Zhang, ""Buddhist Diplomacy: History and Status Quo."

84 Buddhistdoor Global, "The Global Buddhist Congregation 2011."
85 Lewis, "India Plans 'First-Ever' Global Buddhist Conference in November."
86 Lewis, "India Plans 'First-Ever' Global Buddhist Conference in November."
87 Curanović, *The Religious Diplomacy of the Russian Federation*, 6–7.
88 Nye, "Get Smart: Combining Hard and Soft Power," 160.
89 Haass and O'Sullivan, "Terms of Engagement: Alternatives to Punitive Policies."
90 Traub, "The Hillary Clinton Doctrine."
91 Lee, "Clinton: Islam, West Can Agree on Tolerance."
92 Walker and Ludwig, "From 'Soft Power' to 'Sharp Power': Rising Authoritarian Influence in the Democratic World," 17. See also Nye, "How Sharp Power Threatens Soft Power," where the author argues that sharp power is a type of hard power.
93 Kourgiotis, "'Moderate Islam' Made in the United Arab Emirates."
94 Reisen, Soto, and Weithöner, "Financing Global and Regional Public Goods Through ODA: Analysis and Evidence from the OECD Creditor Reporting System," 11.
95 Lee, "Clinton: Islam, West Can Agree on Tolerance."
96 Yilmaz and Barry, "Instrumentalizing Islam in a 'Secular' State," 4–5.
97 Patranobis, "China Angry at Dalai Lama's Nalanda Visit, Says Move Could Disrupt Ties with India." Regarding the location of the above cases on the ID-PD Radar, see footnote 28.
98 USAID, "2020 Evidence Summit."
99 Beck, "Turkey's Global Soft-Power Push Is Built on Mosques."
100 Hanson, "Ankara to Host Interfaith Dialogue Expo as Hagia Sophia Controversy Heats Up."
101 Kalra and Deshmukh, "Assessing the Status of Hagia Sophia as a 'Mosque' under the UNESCO Convention."
102 UN News, "UNESCO Expresses Deep Regret over Turkey Decision to Change Status of Historic Hagia Sophia."
103 "Turkey Says UNESCO's Remarks on Hagia Sophia Mosque 'Biased,'" *Hürriyet Daily News*, July 24, 2021.
104 DW.com, "Turkey Hits Back at UNESCO Concern over Hagia Sophia."
105 UN News, "UNESCO Expresses Deep Regret."
106 Erbay, "TIKA President Serdar Çam: Turkey Keeps Breaking Records in Humanitarian Aid and Development Assistance."
107 Yilmaz and Barry, "Instrumentalizing Islam in a 'Secular' State," 7–10.
108 Çevik, "Reassessing Turkey's Soft Power: The Rules of Attraction."
109 Walker and Ludwig, "A Full-Spectrum Response to Sharp Power: The Vulnerabilities and Strengths of Open Societies," 3.
110 Kalin, "Turkey's Smart Power."
111 "Putin Communicates with Erdogan on Hagia Sophia," *Orthodox Times*.
112 Hanson, "Ankara to Host Interfaith Dialogue Expo."

113 BBC News, "Hagia Sophia: World Council of Churches Appeals to Turkey on Mosque Decision."
114 Yükleyen, "Compatibility of 'Islam' and 'Europe': Turkey's EU Accession."
115 Tarusarira, "Religion and Coloniality in Diplomacy," 87.
116 Buddhistdoor Global, "Indonesia Aims to Promote Borobudur as a Global Buddhist Travel Destination."
117 Khaliq, "Religious and Cultural Tourism to the Ancient Gandhara Region Promotes Multiculturalism, Interfaith Harmony and Peace."

REFERENCES

Agrawal, Sandeep, and Caitlin Barratt. "Does Proximity Matter in Promoting Interfaith Dialogue?" *Journal of International Migration and Integration* 15, no. 3 (2014): 567–587.

Al-Monitor. "Ankara to Host Interfaith Dialogue Expo as Hagia Sophia Controversy Heats Up," August 3, 2020. https://www.al-monitor.com/originals/2020/08/turkey-exhibition-on-dialogue-osman-kavala-hagia-sophia.html#ixzz76l38irky.

Arab News. "Saudi Arabia Taking Lead in Interfaith Dialogue," September 22, 2018. https://www.arabnews.com/node/1376336/saudi-arabia.

Associated Press, "Saudi King Calls for End to Islamic Extremism," June 5, 2008. https://www.nbcnews.com/id/wbna24970557

Baker, Nigel. "Religion and Diplomacy: A British View from the Vatican." *Church, Communication and Culture* 1, no. 1 (2016): 255–267.

Barua, Dipen, "Indonesia Aims to Promote Borobudur as a Global Buddhist Travel Destination." *Buddhistdoor*, July 19, 2021. https://www.buddhistdoor.net/news/indonesia-aims-to-promote-borobudur-as-a-global-buddhist-travel-destination

BBC News. "Hagia Sophia: World Council of Churches appeals to Turkey on mosque decision," July 11, 2020. https://www.bbc.com/news/world-europe-53375739.

Beck, John M. "Turkey's Global Soft-Power Push Is Built on Mosques." *The Atlantic*, June 1, 2019. https://www.theatlantic.com/international/archive/2019/06/turkey-builds-mosques-abroad-global-soft-power/590449/.

Bertrand, Gilles. "Turkish Diplomacy since 2003: Transition from Realpolitik to a Liberal Foreign Policy?" *Perspectives: Review of Central European Affairs* 2 (2013): 63–82.

Boao Forum for Asia. "About BFA." n.d. https://english.boaoforum.org/about.html.

Buddhist Door, "The Global Buddhist Congregation 2011," December 1, 2011. https://www.buddhistdoor.net/features/the-global-buddhist-congregation-2011.

Burley, Mikel. "Narrative Philosophy of Religion: Apologetic and Pluralistic orientations." *International Journal for Philosophy of Religion* 88, no. 1 (2020): 5–21.

Cancel, Amanda E., Michael A. Mitrook, and Glen T. Cameron. "Testing the Contingency Theory of Accommodation in Public Relations." *Public Relations Review* 25, no. 2 (1999): 171–197.

CARPO. "Iran-Saudi Dialogue Initiative". n.d. https://carpo-bonn.org/en/iran-saudi-dialogue-initiative/.

Çevik, Senem B. "Reassessing Turkey's Soft Power: The Rules of Attraction." *Alternatives* 44, no. 1 (2019): 50–71.

China Committee on Religion and Peace. "About CCRP." n.d. http://www.cppcc.gov.cn/ccrp/zzhyw/syyw/.

China News Service. "Representatives of Religions and Peace Organizations from around the World Explore Interfaith Collaboration to Combat Corona Virus Pandemic," October 12, 2020. http://k.sina.com.cn/article_1784473157_6a5ce645020020lh2.html.

Chu, Lan T. "Vatican Diplomacy in China and Vietnam." In *Religion and Public Diplomacy*, pp. 57–73. Palgrave Macmillan, New York, 2013.

Curanović, Alicja. "The Religious Diplomacy of the Russian Federation." *Russia/NIS Center Report,* no. 12 (2012). https://www.ifri.org/sites/default/files/atoms/files/ifrirnr12curanovicreligiousdiplomacyjune2012.pdf.

Do, Je Hae. "Korea's Isolated Buddhism Opening Doors." *Korea Times*, December 27, 2011. https://m.koreatimes.co.kr/pages/article.asp?newsIdx=101660&KK.

Doyle, Michael, and Stefano Recchia. "Liberalism in International Relations." In *International Encyclopedia of Political Science*, edited by B. Badie, D. Berg-Schlosser, and L. Morlino, 1435–1439. Thousand Oaks: SAGE Publications Inc, 2011.

DW. "Turkey Hits Back at UNESCO Concern over Hagia Sophia," July 24, 2021. https://www.dw.com/en/turkey-hits-back-at-unesco-concern-over-hagia-sophia/a-58626501.

Erbay, Nur Özkan. "TIKA President Serdar Çam: Turkey Keeps Breaking Records in Humanitarian Aid and Development aAssistance." *Daily Sabah*, December 10, 2018. https://www.dailysabah.com/politics/2018/12/10/tika-president-serdar-cam-turkey-keeps-breaking-records-in-humanitarian-aid-and-development-assistance.

Evans, Alex, and David Steven. "Towards a Theory of Influence for Twenty-first Century Foreign Policy: The New Public Diplomacy in a Globalized World." *Place Branding and Public Diplomacy* 6, no. 1 (2010): 18–26.

Fahy, John. "International Relations and Faith-Based Diplomacy: The Case of Qatar." *The Review of Faith & International Affairs* 16, no. 3 (2018): 76–88.

Fitzgerald, Michael Louis. "Vatican II and Interfaith Dialogue." In *Interfaith Dialogue*, edited by Edmund Kee-Fook Chia, 3–15. New York: Palgrave Macmillan, 2016.

Frieden, Jeffry. A., and David. A. Lake. "Introduction: International Politics and International Economics. In *International Political Economy*, edited by Jeffry. A. Frieden and David. A. Lake, 11–26. Boston: Routledge, 2002.

G20 Interfaith Forum, "About G20 Interfaith Forum." https://www.g20interfaith.org/g20-interfaith-forum-about/.

General Assembly of the United Nations. "Culture of Peace: High-level Dialogue on Interreligious and Intercultural Understanding and Cooperation for Peace." https://www.un.org/en/ga/62/plenary/peaceculturehld/bkg.shtml.

Griffin, Em, Ledbetter, Andrew, and Sparks, Glenn. *A First Look at Communication Theory* (10th edition). New York: McGraw-Hill, 2019.

Grunig, James E. "Two-way Symmetrical Public Relations: Past, Present, and Future." In *Handbook of public relations*, edited by R.L. Heath, 11–30. Thousand Oaks: Sage, 2001.

Grunig, James E., and David M. Dozier. *Excellent Public Relations and Effective Organizations: A Study of Communication Management in Three Countries*. New York: Routledge, 2003.

Grunig, James E., and Jon White. "The Effect of Worldviews on Public Relations Theory and Practice." In *Excellence in Public Relations and Communication Management*, edited by James E. Grunig, 31-64. Hillsdale, NJ: Lawrence Erlbaum Associates, 1992.

Guler, Sena. "Turkey Slams FETO Terror Group-backed Interfaith Dialogue Project in Germany." *Anadolu Agency*, May 27, 2021. https://www.aa.com.tr/en/turkey/turkey-slams-feto-terror-group-backed-interfaith-dialogue-project-in-germany/2256675.

Haynes, Jeffrey. "The United Nations Alliance of Civilizations and Interfaith Dialogue: What Is It Good For?" *The Review of Faith & International Affairs* 16, no. 3 (2018): 48–60.

Haas, R. N., and Meghan L. O'Sullivan. "Terms of Engagement: Alternatives to Punitive Policies." *Survival* 42, no. 2 (2010): 113–135.

Hanson, Matt A. "Ankara to Host Interfaith Dialogue Expo as Hagia Sophia Controversy Heats Up," August 3, 2020. https://www.al-monitor.com/originals/2020/08/turkey-exhibition-on-dialogue-osman-kavala-hagia-sophia.html#ixzz76NAUtRgq.

Hurriyet Daily News. "Turkey Says UNESCO's Remarks on Hagia Sophia Mosque 'Biased'," July 24, 2021. https://www.hurriyetdailynews.com/turkey-says-unescos-remarks-on-hagia-sophia-mosque-biased-166552.

Hopf, Ted. "The Promise of Constructivism in International Relations Theory." *International Security* 23 (1) (1998): 171–200.

Hunter, Shireen. "How Effective Is Interfaith Dialogue as an Instrument for Bridging International Differences and Achieving Conflict Resolution?" *The Review of Faith & International Affairs* 16, no. 3 (2018): 102–113.

International Quaran News Service. "Iran, Vatican Inter-Religious Dialogue Planned in Tehran." November 9, 2019. https://iqna.ir/en/news/3469834/iran-vatican-inter-religious-dialogue-planned-in-tehran.

Johnston, Douglas. (ed.). *Faith-Based Diplomacy: Trumping Realpolitik*. New York: Oxford University Press, 2003.

Joint Learning Initiative. "International Partnership on Religion & Sustainable Development (PaRD)." n.d. https://jliflc.com/organizations/pard/.

Kalra, Varun and Vishwajeet Deshmukh. "Assessing the Status of Hagia Sophia as a 'Mosque' under the UNESCO Convention," September 2, 2020. https://www.jurist.org/commentary/2020/09/kalra-deshmukh-status-hagia-sophia-as-a-mosque/.

Kalin, Ibrahim. "Turkey's Smart Power," May 8, 2008. https://www.setav.org/en/turkeys-smart-power/.

Keaten, James A, and Charles Soukup. "Dialogue and Religious Otherness: Toward a Model of Pluralistic Interfaith Dialogue." *Journal of international and intercultural communication* 2, no. 2 (2009): 168–187.

Kent, Michael L., and Maureen Taylor. "Building Dialogic Relationships Through the World Wide Web." *Public Relations Review* 24, no. 3 (1998): 321–334.

Kent, Michael L., and Maureen Taylor. "Toward a Dialogic Theory of Public Relations." *Public Relations Review* 28, no. 1 (2002): 21–37.

Khaliq, Fazal. "Religious and Cultural Tourism to the Ancient Gandhara Region Promotes Multiculturalism, Interfaith Harmony and Peace." *Asia Leadership Fellow Program e-magazine* 6 (2020). https://alfpnetwork.jfac.jp/en/wp-content/uploads/2020/04/ALFP-e-magazine-6-article-2-Fazal-Khaliq_PDF-version.pdf.

Knitter, Paul. "A Common Creation Story? Interreligious Dialogue and Ecology." *Journal of Ecumenical Studies* 37, no. 3-4 (2000): 285–300.

Kourgiotis, Panos. "'Moderate Islam' Made in the United Arab Emirates: Public Diplomacy and the Politics of Containment." *Religions* 11, no. 1(2020), 1–17.

Lee, Matthew, "Clinton: Islam, West Can Agree on Tolerance." *Associated Press*, July 15, 2011. https://www.victoriaadvocate.com/news/nation/clinton-islam-west-can-agree-on-tolerance/article_38d632ee-a528-5a13-b493-114829dc7c9b.html.

Lews, Craig. "India Plans 'First-Ever' Global Buddhist Conference in November." *Buddhist Door*, September 15, 2021. https://www.buddhistdoor.net/news/india-plans-first-ever-global-buddhist-conference-in-november.

Long, David, and Frances Woolley. "Global Public Goods: Critique of a UN Discourse." *Global Governance* 15, no. 1 (2009): 107-122.

Mao, Lijun, "Inclusiveness, Mutual Learning, and Collaboration among Ten-Thousands of States: The Wisdom and Mission of Religion on the Belt and Route." *The CPPCC News*. April 22, 2021. http://www.cppcc.gov.cn/ccrp/2021/04/22/ARTI1619060068954295.shtml.

McDonagh, Philip, Lucia Vázquez Mendoza, Kishan Manocha, and John Neary. *On the Significance of Religion for Global Diplomacy*. New York: Routledge, 2020.

Murphy, Priscilla. "The Limits of Symmetry: A Game Theory Approach to Symmetric and Asymmetric Public Relations." *Journal of Public Relations Research* 3, no. 1–4 (1991): 115-131.

Musa, Mohammad Alami. "Inter-faith Dialogue in Singapore Must Go Deeper." *The Strait Times*, October 27, 2017. https://www.straitstimes.com/opinion/inter-faith-dialogue-in-singapore-must-go-deeper.

National News. "Inter-religious Meeting for Dialogue and World Peace Wraps Up in Havana," October 19, 2015. https://www.radiohc.cu/en/noticias/nacionales/73099-inter-religious-meeting-for-dialogue-and-world-peace-wraps-up-in-havana.

Neufeldt, Reina C. "Interfaith Dialogue: Assessing Theories of Change." *Peace & Change* 36, no. 3 (2011): 344-372.

Nye, Joseph. "Get Smart: Combining Hard and Soft Power." *Foreign Affairs*, July/August (2009). https://www.foreignaffairs.com/artic les/2009-07-01/get-smart.

Nye, Joseph. "Hard, Soft, and Smart Power." In *The Oxford Handbook of Modern Diplomacy*, edited by Edited by Andrew F. Cooper, Jorge Heine, and Ramesh Thakur, 559-574. Oxford: Oxford University Press, 2013.

Nye, Joseph. "How Sharp Power Threatens Soft Power." *Foreign Affairs*, January (2018). https://www.foreignaffairs.com/articles/china /2018-01-24/how-sharp-power-threatens-soft-power.

Obama White House Archives. "Promoting Interfaith Dialogue and Cooperation." n.d. https://obamawhitehouse.archives.gov/administration/eop/ofbnp/policy/interfaith.

Ociepka, Beata. "Public diplomacy as Political Communication: Lessons from Case Studies." *European Journal of Communication* 33, no. 3 (2018): 290–303.

OECD Development Center. "Financing Global and Regional Public Goods through ODA: Analysis and Evidence from the OECD Creditor Reporting System." *Working Paper,* No. 232 (2004). https://www.oecd.org/dev/pgd/24482500.pdf.

Orthodox Times. "Putin Communicates with Erdogan on Hagia Sophia," July 13, 2020. https://orthodoxtimes.com/putin-communicates-with-erdogan-on-hagia-sophia/.

Payne, J. Gregory. "Reflections on Public Diplomacy: People-to-People Communication." *American Behavioral Scientist* 53, no. 4 (2009): 579–606.

Patranobis, Sutirtho. "China Angry at Dalai Lama's Nalanda Visit, Says Move Could Disrupt Ties with India." *Hindustan Times*, March 21, 2017. https://www.hindustantimes.com/world-news/china-angry-at-dalai-lama-s-nalanda-visit-says-india-acting-against-core-concern/story-b2y9bn8Hft68Fd2GPrbyJK.html.

Pew Research Center. "Religious Hostilities Reach Six-year High," January 14, 2014. https://www.pewforum.org/2014/01/14/religious-hostilities-reach-six-year-high/.

Pope, Elizabeth M. "'This Is a Head, Hearts, and Hands Enterprise': Adult Learning in Interfaith Dialogue." *Adult Education Quarterly* 70, no. 3 (2020): 205–222.

Plowman, Kenneth D., William G. Briggs, and Yi-Hui Huang. "Public Relations and Conflict Resolution." In *Handbook of public relations*, edited by Robert L. Heath, 301–310. Thousand Oaks, California: SAGE Publications,Inc., 2001.

Radio Free Europe. "U.S.: Undersecretary of State Pushes for More Interfaith Dialogue," June 11, 2006.https://www.rferl.org/a/1069072.html.

Reuters. "Austria to Shut Saudi-backed Religious Dialogue Center in Rights Protest," June 12, 2019. https://www.reuters.com/article/us-austria-saudi/austria-to-shut-saudi-backed-religious-dialogue-center-in-rights-protest-idUSKCN1TD2DR.

Russian Orthodox Church. "Statement of Russian Orthodox Church's Holy Synod Concerning Decision of Turkish Authorities to Change Status of Hagia Sophia," July 17, 2020. http://www.patriarchia.ru/en/db/text/5664223.html.

Russian Orthodox Church. "Members of Interreligious Council in Russia meet with Mr. Miguel Angel Moratinos, UN Under-Secretary-General, High Representative for Alliance of Civilizations," January 22, 2021. http://www.patriarchia.ru/en/db/text/5760730.html.

Saragih, Hendra Maujana, Esca Hutama Prayogo Surya, and Syifa Nur Islamiah. "Indonesia's Effort to Improve Islamic Images in The United States During 2009-2017: A Case Study of Interfaith Dialogue." *AJIS: Academic Journal of Islamic Studies* 5, no. 1 (2020): 1–20.

Sherlock, Richard. "Religiosity as a Public Good." *Politics and the Life Sciences* 27, no. 2 (2008): 2–12.

Swedish Water House, "Value Water: Interfaith Statement on Water and Faith from the SIWI Swedish Water House Cluster group," September 24, 2020. https://programme.worldwaterweek.org/Content/ProposalResources/PDF/2021/pdf-2021-9863-1-Interfaith-Statement-on-Water-and-Faith_ENG.pdf.

Tarusarira, Joram. "Religion and Coloniality in Diplomacy." *The Review of Faith & International Affairs* 18, no. 3 (2020): 87–96.

The Korean Times. "Buddhists Regret China's Boycott of World Conference," June 14, 2012. https://www.koreatimes.co.kr/www/culture/2021/05/135_113083.html.

Theunissen, Petra, and Wan Norbani Wan Noordin. "Revisiting the Concept 'Dialogue' in Public Relations." *Public Relations Review* 38, no. 1 (2012): 5–13.

The White House. "Fact Sheet: President Biden Reestablishes the White House Office of Faith-Based and Neighborhood Partnerships," February 21, 2021. https://www.whitehouse.gov/briefing-room/statements-releases/2021/02/14/fact-sheet-president-biden-reestablishes-the-white-house-office-of-faith-based-and-neighborhood-partnerships/.

Traub, James. "The Hilary Clinton Doctrine." *Foreign Policy*, November (2015). https://foreignpolicy.com/2015/11/06/hillary-clinton-doctrine-obama-interventionist-tough-minded-president/.

UN News. "UNESCO Expresses Deep Regret over Turkey Decision to Change Status of Historic Hagia Sophia," July 10, 2020. https://news.un.org/en/story/2020/07/1068151.

USAID. "U.S. Sponsors Bangladesh Conference for Religious and Community Leaders on Advancing Development in Asia," Mar 19, 2010. https://www.prnewswire.com/news-releases/us-sponsors-bangladesh-conference-for-religious-and-community-leaders-on-advancing-development-in-asia-88689152.html.

USAID, "2020 Evidence Summit on Strategic Religious Engagement," April 28, 2021. https://www.usaid.gov/faith-and-opportunity-initiatives/2020-evidence-summit-strategic-religious-engagement.

US Department of State. "Jakarta Interfaith Event," January 25, 2010. https://2009-2017.state.gov/r/pa/prs/ps/2010/01/136491.htm

Walker, Christopher and Jessica Ludwig. "The Meaning of Sharp Power: How Authoritarian States Project Influence." In *Sharp Power: Rising Authoritarian Influence*, edited by The International Forum for Democratic Studies, 8–25. National Endowment for Democracy, 2017. https://www.ned.org/wp-content/uploads/2017/12/Sharp-Power-Rising-Authoritarian-Influence-Full-Report.pdf.

Walker, Christopher and Jessica Ludwig. "A Full-Spectrum Response to Sharp Power: The Vulnerabilities and Strengths of Open Societies." The International Forum for Democratic Studies, 2021. https://www.ned.org/wp-content/uploads/2021/06/A-Full-Spectrum-Response-to-Sharp-Power-The-Vulnerabilities-and-Strengths-of-Open-Societies-Walker-Ludwig-June-2021.pdf.

Wilson, Peter. "Idealism in International Relations." In *Encyclopedia of Power*, edited by Keith Dowding, 332–356. Thousand Oaks: SAGE Publications Inc., 2011.

World Council of Churches. "Interfaith Statement on Climate Change," September 21, 2014. https://www.oikoumene.org/resources/documents/interfaith-statement-on-climate-change.

Yilmaz, Ihsan, and James Barry. "Instrumentalizing Islam in a 'Secular State': Turkey's Diyanet and Interfaith Dialogue." *Journal of Balkan and Near Eastern Studies* 22, no. 1 (2020): 1-16.

Yukleyen, Ahmet. "Compatibility of 'Islam' and 'Europe': Turkey's EU Accession." *Insight Turkey* 11, no. 1 (2009): 115–131.

Zhang, Juyan. "Compassion versus Manipulation; Narratives versus Rational Arguments: a PD Radar to Chart the Terrain of Public Diplomacy." *Place Branding and Public Diplomacy* 16(1) (2020): 195-211.

Zhang, Juyan, and Brecken Chinn Swartz. "Public Diplomacy to Promote Global Public Goods (GPG): Conceptual Expansion, Ethical Grounds, and Rhetoric." *Public Relations Review* 35, no. 4 (2009): 382-387.

Zhang, Juyan. "Buddhist Diplomacy: History and Status Quo." *CPD Perspective*, no. 7 (2012). https://uscpublicdiplomacy.org/sites/uscpublicd iplomacy.org /files/useruploads/u35361/2012%20Paper%208.pdf.

SHARON ROSEN

BRIDGING THE DIVIDES
Interreligious Diplomacy for Effective Peacebuilding

INTRODUCTION

Until recently, most Western secular societies eschewed engagement with religious actors and institutions when it comes to solving conflicts in the field of international diplomacy. Scarred by the violent conflicts of previous centuries, religion has generally been perceived as part of the problem and the marriage of religion and political power an unholy union causing great devastation and needing clear separation. Both the United States and France enshrined this separation in their constitutions, and while the queen or king remains the titular head of the Anglican Church, their purely constitutional roles ensure that religious and political power remain separate in the United Kingdom.

But the popular belief that religion is in its death throes in the face of secular, technological globalization has been challenged in recent years as states increasingly acknowledge that religion still plays a dominant role in many societies around the world. Research has demonstrated that religion is not the main cause of war,[1] but at the same time, the majority of armed conflicts have a religious dimension—and that number is growing.[2] The oft-quoted Pew report that more than four-fifths of the world's inhabitants identify with a religious community—with an upward projection over the next decades—was startling to many in the secular West, although it was met with less surprise in more traditional societies where religion and religious leaders play a highly significant role in people's lives and in setting social norms.[3]

In 2001, the shocking attacks of September 11 focused the world's attention on the role religion—or, more accurately, the abuse of religion—can play as a weapon of violent conflict. Calls for countering or preventing violent extremism, with concomitant descriptions of "religious fundamentalists and extremists," proliferated in policy analyses as governments developed even greater numbers of security tools for their arsenals. This, together, with the growing persecution of religious minorities in more and more countries, has tended to encourage a binary framing of religious actors as either aggressive perpetrators or victimized minorities. In turn, this objectifying of religious people and problems has influenced international policymakers' considerations on whether to engage religious actors in diplomacy to advance peacebuilding.

The above narrative is, however, being seriously challenged both by a growing number of policymakers who acknowledge the failure of present policies to curtail violence and by the increasing recognition of religious actors' potential to positively influence outcomes as part of the solution. It is also now recognized, particularly since COVID-19 has reared its ugly head and caused such mental, emotional, physical, and spiritual devastation globally, that religious leaders are often among the most trusted and influential members in communities.[4] They provide succor, a sense of stability, and spiritual support during these uncertain times, which are likely to continue for some years. They also have multi-religious assets at their disposal, are often the first to respond to needs within their communities, and their influence can extend beyond their communities if they are provided with the skills and the opportunities to act accordingly.

RELIGION: THE PROBLEM AND THE SOLUTION

To be clear, religion does have the power to be both a force for peace and a weapon of war. For believers, religion is an inextricable and profound part of their identity, an identity marker at the most existential level of their being, both individually and communally. Identity plays a highly significant role in the intersection between religion and conflict because when people feel that their deeply held religious identities or "their God" is under attack, they tend to withdraw into their communities, demonize the other, and find reasons to justify violence as defense of their beliefs. Religion then becomes a lightning rod that can be manipulated to galvanize people into violent conflict for their country, nation, land, community, and family.

Given the above alternative, it makes sense to engage religious actors as a force for peace, and indeed, there are already many religious leaders who are acting as an important part of the solution, rather than the problem. They work to reduce conflicts and help those suffering from violence and oppression in their communities. They also participate in the thousands of faith-based and first responder organizations around the world. The sacred texts of all religions declare peace a supreme value.

The overriding motivations that lead to violent conflict can be reduced to several very human traits and emotions: the pursuit of power, greed, selfishness, dehumanization, as well as fear, anger and past traumas. Changing that behavior requires a cultural and spiritual transformation that can be sourced in religious texts through messages that encourage caring for the vulnerable; sharing bread with the hungry; welcoming the stranger; greater awareness, betterment, and appreciation of self and other; eternal hope; and belief in human dignity as a manifestation of the divine.

However—and here comes the catch—these texts need to be internalized by adherents in their universalistic as well as personal sense; they need to be understood as applying to all people and not just members of a specific religion. That is the gauntlet that religious actors need to pick up if they are to play their role in interreligious diplomacy for peacebuilding effectively.

SEARCH FOR COMMON GROUND: VALUES AND ACTIVITIES

At Search for Common Ground (Search), my professional home for the past seventeen years, I have observed these changing patterns of opinions up close. While I personally have worked on religious engagement projects throughout my time at Search, the organization only began pursuing a prioritized strategic approach to engaging religious actors in peacebuilding five years ago when I was appointed as the first director of religious engagement. As the leading international organization dedicated to peacebuilding and with offices in Africa, Asia, and the Middle East—locations where religion plays a significant role in people's lives—we have naturally engaged with religious actors on locally designed and implemented projects. We could hardly have done otherwise and still be effective in our peacemaking mission. One successful project that comes to mind is the establishment, in cooperation with Morocco's Ministry of Justice, of an Alternative Dispute Resolution (ADR) program that blends Islamic texts with contemporary ADR techniques and that has been implemented by imams in prison services. Another initiative involved engaging religious leaders in the Central African Republic in efforts to transform violent extremism and build social cohesion.

Another project, different from the previous ones because of its global scope, is the development and implementation of a Universal Code of Conduct on Holy Sites (Universal Code). Formulated over a period of fifteen years in collaboration with faith-based organizations and senior religious leaders of all faiths, the Universal Code's purpose is to safeguard holy sites from attack and enable adherents to freely access and pray at their sacred spaces.[5] Aligned with the UN's plan of action to protect holy sites,[6] the Universal Code has been implemented in diverse locations from Nigeria to the Balkans to the Holy Land. At its heart is a peacebuilding diplomatic role religious leaders play on an issue that is of common interest to all religious adherents.

However, until recently, Search's projects with a religious component relied mostly on the local knowledge of field staff and their ability to recruit religious people among their participants. Five years ago, as opinions from some policymakers were beginning to emerge about the need to engage religious actors in reducing conflict more consciously, systematically, and with greater religious literacy, Search, a secular organization, began a journey to develop a strategic cross-cutting approach to religious engagement as a theme across the organization. The approach, based on common ground values of peacebuilding, became the foundation for a religious engagement toolkit for Search's thousand-member staff. Our aim was to learn how to be more religiously literate and confident in working with religious actors across the board, both intrareligiously and interreligiously, in order to make us more effective in reaching our peacebuilding goals.

The Common Ground Approach (CGA) to religious engagement is built on three assumptions:

1. Religious actors have the influence and knowledge to shape norms in their communities and in their societies and are members of institutions that can scale positive change. Therefore, it is vital to involve them interreligiously in peacebuilding, particularly on conflicts that have a religious dimension, if we want to be effective in reducing violence.
2. Because religion has the power to be both a force for peace and a weapon of war, engaging religious actors is essential if we want to maximize the former and minimize the latter.
3. Applying a CGA that values dialogue, collaboration, and inclusion as an accepted response to reducing violent conflict will result in effectively finding ways to reach practical win-win solutions across religious dividing lines.

When we at Search talk about "common ground values," we are referring to five foundational principles that inform our activities:

collaboration, audacity, tenacity, empathy, and results. Especially with regard to religious engagement initiatives, we focus on collaboration that includes men, women, and young people within and across religions and sectors; maintaining hope by persistently trying out new and creative paths in the face of obstacles; being nimble, adaptive, and ready for the long haul; listening deeply and offering empathy, whether we agree or not; and concretely making a difference with positive results. The similarities between the above five principles and those needed for successful diplomacy are striking.

It is important to distinguish between interreligious dialogue and interreligious diplomacy. The former is a prerequisite for the latter but can stand independently of it. Its purpose is to share spiritual and moral values, knowledge, appreciation for one's own religion and others, and interfaith relationships of trust and friendship among religious actors. There is no contradiction here with Pope Francis's encyclical, *Fratelli Tutti*, in which he states, "Dialogue between the followers of different religions does not take place simply for the sake of diplomacy, consideration or tolerance."[7] However, if the purpose is specifically peacebuilding in conflict torn regions, particularly where the conflict has a religious dimension, then interreligious dialogue becomes a means towards a peaceful outcome through interreligious diplomacy.

CHALLENGES OF WORKING WITH RELIGIOUS ACTORS

There are challenges, however, to working with religious actors, including the following:

Exclusion: How do you maintain values of inclusion when, for historical, social, cultural, and, in some cases, theological reasons, religions are overwhelmingly patriarchal, with men maintaining power and authority over women and young people? As with changing cultural mores, the insistence on equal human rights for peoples in all their diversity is beginning to effect change in religious communities, but the process is slow and may take generations. Conflicts around gender roles and norms in religion generally reflect the place of a society on a continuum between tradition and modernity. Religions have a tradition of studying and interpreting holy texts, so the more societies are exposed to a diversity of leadership roles and cultures, the more likely they are to interpret traditional texts in new ways.

At Search we generally use the term religious "actors" rather than religious "leaders" in order to highlight the fact that religious leaders do not necessarily need to hold formal religious authority, titles, or qualifications, which are often unavailable to women and young people. They also include individuals in society—men, women, and youth—who exercise influence within a religious community by virtue of their standing, credibility, and activities.

Interestingly, research also suggests that "for a large and growing segment of young people, religiosity is increasingly decoupled from institutions, even as they express high levels of religious belief, practice and identity."[8] Over 75% of young people identify as religious or spiritual but do not identify with religious institutions. Are we now seeing a growing reaction in our societies against the fusion of religious authority with male power, similar to when religious authority is married to political power?

On a positive note, women and youth played a highly prominent role in the two Religions for Peace global meetings in Lindau, Germany, in 2020 and 2021.[9] The Religions for Peace World Council comprises senior religious leaders from all the world's religions, and its 2019 selection of a Muslim woman, Professor Azza Karam, as its Secretary-General reflects the winds of change.

Religious Absolutism: Similar issues arise when religious actors believe that their religion embodies the absolute and exclusive truth—that "God is on their side," and that their interpretation of the truth is the only one. It can be difficult to bring people, in all their diversity, to the table. Interreligious diplomacy, in its essence, calls for the convening of people in conflict from diverse faiths in order to build trusting relationships. Diplomacy does not call for religious actors to surrender their beliefs for the sake of peace and harmony, but it does challenge them to examine how exclusive interpretations of religion may be detrimental to society as a whole and lead to violence. Interreligious dialogue is that first step towards diplomacy, helping people to see commonalities and joint interests amidst religious differences. Once those common interests are uncovered, they can become a launchpad for finding the solutions needed to solve conflict.

Religion and violent extremism: Despite views to the contrary, religions do not advocate violence. Religious people generally are highly sensitive to this assumed connection between religion and violent extremism and see the link as a denigration of their beliefs. They also perceive this link as going hand in hand with heightened discrimination, hate speech, and violence against entire religious communities because of the actions of a small minority. That said, religious actors need to acknowledge that religious discourse, together with violent interpretations, can be and has been coopted by extremists who believe they are carrying out the word of God. It is difficult to envisage religious actors working effectively in the field of interreligious diplomacy if they do not recognize that extremism can emanate from their religions.

There are further challenges here; on the one hand, sensitive and appropriate language needs to be used in diplomacy when discussing violent extremism so that religious actors do not feel the need to defend their religion against attack and blame. On the other hand, religious diplomacy might indeed need the engagement of religious actors with extremist views for effective peacebuilding.

All too often we find ourselves sitting at the table with "the converted" rather than those whose beliefs can lead or have led to violent acts against others. There is a fine line between talking directly with extremists in the hope of peaceful change and legitimizing extremist discourse and action. This dilemma requires careful handling, especially as it can be extremely difficult to maintain the trust of victims of violence while also engaging the perpetrators of that violence.

Instrumentalization: Sometimes governments, policymakers, and other organizations recruit actors, particularly senior religious leaders who have international reach, on diplomatic missions in order to promote an agenda or idea. Using a political leader in such a role might make the approach too formal or publicly known, particularly if the desire is to informally sound out the views of the other side. Such a mission with religious leaders often takes place discreetly and without fanfare and can be very useful for advancing diplomatic steps in peacemaking.

However, political and religious leaders sometimes use one another for their own personal benefit and not for the good of society as a whole, perhaps to promote a specific agenda, gain resources for themselves or their community, or simply to raise a personal profile. Actions like these are counterproductive, as they do not engage the full range of religious voices which, in turn, eliminates some of the complexities and nuance of the dialogue. Bad-faith dialogues can also lower the credibility of religious leaders inside their own communities if, as a result of this instrumentalization, they take an opposing stand to their followers.

Cookie-cutter approaches: When using interreligious diplomacy as a means for peacebuilding, it is vital to know the religious context. Search is currently working on religious engagement projects in twenty countries, and each one is a world to its own. For example, Search is a member of a consortium of secular and faith-based non-governmental organizations called The Joint Initiative for Strategic Religious Action (JISRA) that is funded by the Dutch government. JISRA is an interfaith partnership that lobbies and advocates for Freedom of Religion or Belief (FoRB) in seven countries, including Iraq, Indonesia, and several African countries. Its purpose is to support religious actors' capacity to engage in dialogue, to build interreligious respect for FoRB, and to further its advocacy nationally and internationally. JISRA engages in similar cross-cutting processes (such as intrareligious discussion, interreligious dialogue leading to joint action, and strengthening the voices of women, youth, and religious minorities) in all seven countries, but implementation takes on strikingly different forms in each context.

Another consideration is potential sensitivity in a particular country to focusing on religion. The words "Interreligious Freedom" or "Religious Advocacy" in the title of a project may be off-putting to certain governments and cause concomitant difficulties for the organization that proposes it. Wherever the location, there is a need for a thorough analysis of the context before engaging religious actors.

Untrained Staff: Search staff needed increased religious literacy in order to engage effectively and confidently with religious actors while aligning this literacy to the values of the organization. By "religious literacy," I refer not only to an understanding of the basic precepts of religions, as people's familiarity with religion tends to only extend to their own, but also of religious sensitivities. How does one address religious actors, use religious language codes appropriately, provide for the various religious needs of different populations, or assess when topics can be opened for discussion in intrareligious, interreligious, and cross-sectoral meetings? These are just some of many issues that must be considered. We have discovered that the need for religious literacy is not unique to Search and its staff, but rather is a necessity among policymakers, civil society practitioners, and just about anyone who is interested in effectively partnering with religious communities and organizations.

As a result of this final challenge in particular, one of my top priorities has been the development of *The Common Ground Approach to Religious Engagement*, a training toolkit based on Search's foundational values that was launched in 2020 with support from GHR Foundation, and which is freely available on Search's website in English, French, and Arabic.[10] This was followed by a collaboration between Search and the United States Institute of Peace (USIP) on a free online course, titled "Religious Engagement and Peacebuilding - A Common Ground Approach," which was launched through the USIP Global Academy platform in July 2021, again with GHR's support.[11] The course has proved extremely popular and was adapted into French and Arabic versions six months later.

FREEDOM OF RELIGION OR BELIEF

Peaceful societies are those that are safe, healthy, and just; where members have their basic needs met; where beliefs and values are upheld; and where hopes and aspirations can be fulfilled. After the horrific destruction and devastation of World War II, the Universal Declaration of Human Rights in 1948, attempted to create a universal standard for the protection of rights for all peoples and nations. The Declaration, adopted by the UN General Assembly, included within it the right to freedom of thought, conscience, and religion for all (i.e., the right to practice one's belief, as well as the right *not* to believe as a fundamental requisite for peaceful coexistence). At their essence, peaceful societies protect all human rights and enable diversity to flourish. When religious freedom is threatened, social cohesion suffers, and conflict grows.

Attacks on religious freedom sadly continue apace, and recent reports on Christianity as the most persecuted religion in the world have heightened awareness and freed up resources, particularly from the U.S. and other Western countries, to highlight and improve the situation.[12]

There is a trend that views the rights of religious freedom as inimical to women's, children's, LGBTQI rights or the right to freely express one's disbelief in a religion. Given the risks mentioned above regarding religious exclusionism and absolutism, this is understandable. Conversely, there are those who see the right to practice one's religion as superior to all other rights. The work on FoRB that Search implements in various conflict regions enables us to highlight the interconnection between these rights and to address intersectional concerns in a "common ground" way. By enabling religious actors to express the fears they have about the perceived breakdown of traditional religious, family, and community relationships and values—and empathizing with them—we open opportunities to explore the way different rights can be used to build peaceful societies—a common interest for all.

SEARCH FOR COMMON GROUND: CASE STUDIES

I will now turn to two case studies that describe the benefits and challenges of this interreligious diplomacy approach and how we have found ways to foster positive relationships and reach concrete results.

1. Kyrgyzstan: Expanding Freedom of Belief or Religion in Central Asia

Search has been active in Central Asia for more than a decade, with a flagship office in Bishkek, Kyrgyzstan that covers our regional programs as well as country specific activities in Kyrgyzstan, Uzbekistan, Kazakhstan, and Tajikistan. The programs focus on enabling collaborative approaches to complex issues like religious freedom, violent extremism, and strengthening inclusive societies and governance in countries that suffer from political, religious, and ethnic tensions.

As a former Soviet country, Kyrgyzstan has a complex relationship with religion and state. The communist ideals that precluded any influence of religion on state matters still find deep roots in the country, with an accompanying view that the state must regulate and control religious groups for the sake of unity and solidarity. With the resurgence of Islam after Kyrgyzstan's independence in 1991, encouraged and supported by outside influences, a profound level of mistrust and fear of religious extremism grew between state authorities and some religious communities with the result that the police, the judiciary, and other state instruments have maintained tight control. As the new millennium progressed, the gap between religious and secular groups widened further, with the former identifying secularism as atheism and the latter equating Islam with extremism and Protestantism with brainwashing. This gap, further exacerbated by the emergence of ISIS, accelerated the urgent need to develop clear parameters around the role of religion in the secular state. With a tenacity spanning years while using a common ground collaborative approach that includes representatives of government authorities, religious leaders and civil society organizations, Search has enabled the fostering of institutional legal reform and a more conducive environment for interreligious acceptance.

Funded by the U.S. State Department, our religious engagement work in Central Asia has generally been framed as a tool for transforming violent extremism using a collaborative methodology that builds on multi-religious and multi-stakeholder dialogue. As parties get to know one another and build trust in each other, changes at the structural level have taken place to enshrine guarantees and protections of religious freedom within the legal framework of the Kyrgyz Republic.

In 2015, we started monitoring and evaluating current practices on religious freedom. Of the Central Asian countries, Kyrgyzstan is considered the most open to religious freedom, but the state has struggled to institutionalize a legal framework that ensures fair trial and judgment of cases related to religious expression and violent extremism. Such fairness is critically needed if the risks of radicalization and extremism among religious marginalized groups are to be reduced. To respond to these risks and establish greater accountability in the judicial system, Search worked with civil society representatives to monitor and document cases where religious groups' rights were violated. Search then worked with judiciary and law enforcement authorities to analyze these cases and detect patterns in violations so that the legal framework could be strengthened.

We also set up a multi-sector working group and smaller working group offshoots where representatives from the government, civil society organizations, and religions regularly met together to discuss trends in religious affairs, exchange views around pressing issues, and seek potential solutions within the legal framework. According to an independent evaluation of the project, this had never happened before due to opposing views among stakeholders and the sensitivity of the topic.[13]

The results of the monitoring laid the groundwork for the development of recommendations for strengthening the legal framework and improving enforcement practices through increased communication between the government and non-governmental stakeholders, including religious actors, on the status and legal framework of religious freedom. Using this collaborative methodology, Search also contributed to the development of the Concept in Support of the State Policy of the Kyrgyz Republic on Religious Affairs for 2021–2026 (known as the State Concept), a vision paper that outlines a legal framework (laws, policies, concepts, state programs, and principles) for implementing religious freedom. This concept recommended a holistic and decentralized governmental approach, a stark contrast to previous, securitized approaches.

A practical commentary/guide to the law entitled *On Freedom of Religion and Religious Organizations in the Kyrgyz Republic* was also developed for judges and lawyers to avoid legal misinterpretations. The guide examines each article of the law and explains its provisions in accordance with the Constitution and is a resource to enhance understanding of religious freedom. Seventy-eight judges participated in workshops using the guide as a key resource. Participants learned about the religious context of Kyrgyzstan as well as laws on freedom of conscience and religion and their place in the Constitution. Participants commented that they had a better understanding of wrongful sentencing and recognized the importance of thinking about people's rights before passing judgment.

The working groups also developed two other publications, one on *Human Rights for Dignified Burial* which contributed to reducing tensions around religious burials; and another which led to amendments in the law on forensic science by the Justice Ministry to include religious expertise.

Despite these efforts, discrimination based on religious grounds remains in Kyrgyzstan, with religious minority communities (e.g., Baptists, Jehovah's Witnesses, Baha'i) facing difficulties when arranging for the burial of their dead in public cemeteries, among other issues.[14] At the local level, communities are vulnerable to religious intolerance because of prejudice and stereotypes rooted in fear, misunderstanding, and distrust of the other. There is much still to be done both within Kyrgyzstan and in Central Asia as a whole.

With this in mind, Search has been instrumental in the creation of a *Central Asia State Policy on Religion Learning Network* that includes cross-sectoral representation of government authorities, religious communities, and civil society organizations from Kyrgyzstan, Uzbekistan, Tajikistan, and Kazakhstan. The network has held some meetings, but there are profound differences in the levels of religious freedom among the four countries. However, if participants develop a sense of ownership, safety, and mutual trust from this cross-sectoral collaboration, the network can become an effective institutionalized mechanism for sharing best practices and addressing religious freedom issues across Central Asia.

The creation of this network is an audacious move, given the history of these four countries, and tenacity will be needed to ensure its sustainability. However, this collaborative, cross-sectoral approach, that includes representatives of religious communities playing a diplomatic role vis-à-vis one another and government authorities, seems to be an effective way of reaching constructive results peacefully. Time will tell.

2. Israel: Jewish-Muslim Interreligious Dialogue and Diplomacy

For the past several years, I have been directing a British government-funded initiative in Israel that engages Jewish and Muslim religious actors, male and female, who after a process of mutual trust building, act as change agents for peace within their religious communities towards a negotiated settlement of the Arab-Israeli conflict. The initiative's main assumption is that, because many of the issues at the heart of the conflict have a religious dimension, it is essential to engage influential religious actors in any process to end it. Disregarding religious beliefs and community interests, or working with those disinclined to finding solutions, has fostered strong religious opposition to agreements in the past; this was the case with the failed Oslo Accords. Indeed, religious discourse continues to be used to exacerbate conflict, justify antagonism, and delegitimize narratives on both sides. Here, our aim is to do the opposite—to build a "religious language" for promoting peace based on interpretations of sacred texts and to implement activities that foster these understandings specifically, but not exclusively, within religious communities in order to create grassroots support for a negotiated peace deal. Crafting a peace accord is still the purview of the political leadership, but without the support of religious people in the region, no agreement will pass muster.

The program includes:

- Studying topics at the heart of the conflict in both intra- and interreligious groupings (e.g., Jerusalem and its holy sites, sanctity of life and land, sovereignty, and attitudes towards minorities in its midst, as well as the meaning of peace).
- Learning from influential religious leaders who have advanced peace outside the region.
- Acquiring skills in mediation and conflict resolution.
- Strengthening the voices of women as religious actors and decision-makers.
- Implementing initiatives to advance peace within religious communities including:
    a. Creating a Muslim-Hebrew online platform Al Minbar-Habima (the Stage)[15] managed by the participants with regular posts, videos and interviews.
    b. Developing a four-part curriculum in Arabic and Hebrew on the two religions and the issues at the heart of the conflict for religious Muslim and Jewish educational institutions that is jointly presented by a Muslim and Jewish participant
    c. Joint lectures given by duos of Jewish and Muslim participants on their project learnings to religious educational institutions

    d. Local projects relevant to participants such as building community cohesion after the violence in May 2021.

Many of the religious actors are people with significant political influence and one woman who was an active participant, now has a highly influential governmental position in Israel's Knesset. The Jewish participants are predominantly from the National Religious stream who feel a profound religious attachment to the land and for the most part support a "greater Israel" approach rather than a two-state solution to the conflict. The Muslim actors are Palestinian citizens of Israel, mostly affiliated with the Islamic Movement (Southern Branch that recognizes Israel's right to exist) and are now represented in the coalition government by the Ra'am Party.

To illustrate how interreligious diplomacy works in this project, I will share a story about one of our Jewish participants. Let us call him Rabbi Joseph. He is in his forties, highly influential—both religiously and politically—and a scholar of Jewish law with hundreds of thousands of followers. Rabbi Joseph has strong religious nationalist views that stem from the belief that the Land of Israel was promised by God to the Jewish people three thousand years ago and now that circumstances have miraculously returned it to their hands, it is the Jewish people's duty to ensure it remains so.

Rabbi Joseph's interest in joining the project stemmed from the realization that his religious political party needs to come up with its own scenario for what relations between Israelis and Palestinians could look like in the future given its refusal to accept a two-state solution. During intrareligious study sessions in the first year of the project, his interpretation of texts placed ownership of the land above the holiness of life and peace, and the supremacy of Jewish life above other peoples—words that clashed with his kind, gentle demeanor.

Nevertheless, at the first interreligious meeting, Rabbi Joseph forged a bond with a learned sheikh around an Iftar dinner.[16] The sheikh, a high school principal, invited the rabbi to speak to his students on religious issues. Rabbi Joseph accepted. Shortly thereafter, we took a group of thirty-four men and women, National Religious and Muslim, to Northern Ireland to build interreligious relationships and to learn lessons from that conflict from senior religious, political, educational, and law enforcement representatives. Rabbi Joseph, born in Israel, did not have a passport believing that once *in situ*, he must never leave the country.

However, after several consultations with rabbis, he applied for a passport and traveled with us. That trip was a turning point for him and many others as they listened, learned, and built relationships.

On their return, the religious actors broke into working groups to decide on what activities they would engage in to expand constituencies for peace. As part of the education group, Rabbi Joseph reported on its decision to work towards reducing violence in schools, both Arab and Jewish; to ensure that each side learns about the other's religious practices and to confront the inequalities in educational standards.

Despite religious differences and the seeming intractability of the Arab/Israeli conflict, interreligious diplomacy has power. It works particularly well with people whose religion holds profound meaning for them because religious commonalities are so easily uncovered—dedication to religious principles and practice, love of God, among others.

I could also tell the story of Aziza, a charismatic Muslim lawyer, dressed in hijab and long coat, whose harsh words against Jewish political and social oppression when we first met, ring in my ears and who, by the third year of the project had developed profound relationships with National Religious women, was presenting joint lectures to religious audiences, and was learning Shari'a law so that she had the "religious language" to discuss issues at the heart of the conflict more confidently with her Jewish counterparts.

Another engaging story is that of Noa, a young National Religious woman from Lod who gave birth to her third child three weeks before the eruption of violence in that mixed Arab-Jewish town in May 2021. Despite her fragile health and the dangerous security situation, she insisted on finding ways to sustain neighborly contact during the violence. She has become a leader in her town, regularly giving joint lectures, together with another participant of ours, a Muslim municipal leader from the neighboring mixed town of Ramleh, on the contrasting ways their towns dealt with the conflict, for good and bad, and on possible ways to build social cohesion.

The project has held on by the skin of its teeth during times of military conflict when people have left in anger and desperation, only to return later, reflecting the resilience of personal relationships. Sometimes there have been internal blow-ups, both intrareligious and interreligious, with some participants permanently leaving. Nevertheless, initial results indicate that interreligious diplomacy can change attitudes and behaviors that, over time and in large enough numbers, can contribute to the fertile ground needed for a sustained agreement to end the Arab-Israeli conflict. This message was highlighted by one of our participants, highly influential both politically and in the public health field, who recently tweeted:

"I participated today in a festive event at the British Ambassador's residence as a member of an interreligious project of Search that totally changed the prism of how I see the (Arab-Israeli) conflict. I am a right-wing National Religious woman but today, with motivation, I also fight for the civil rights of Arab women. There are lots of arguments but also a lot in common—and I will not give up on the commonalities."[17]

CONCLUSION

In a recently published book titled *Interreligious Heroes,* Alon Goshen-Gottstein reflects on the traits of major interreligious actors, past and present, that "sustain the world."[18] While not a definitive list, he points to their ability to build interreligious friendships that enable transformation to occur, to them being caring human beings, flexible and stable, humble and determined, tenacious and courageous, open and curious, empathic, trusting in God and human beings, with a religious authenticity that enables authentic activity for the good of all. These interreligious heroes, men and women, young and old, are the stuff of peacemaking and model a mode of interreligious diplomacy that we must nurture and support.

NOTES
1. Institute for Economics & Peace, "Five Key Questions."
2. Baumann, Finnbogason, and Svensson, "Rethinking Mediation," 1.
3. Hackett, Grim, et al., "The Global Religious Landscape."
4. See also the contribution by Nukhet Sandal in this issue.
5. Universal Code of Conduct on Holy Sites, "About the Code."
6. United Nations Alliance of Civilizations, "The United Nations Plan of Action to Safeguard Religious Sites."
7. Francis, *Fratelli Tutti*.
8. "The State of Religion & Young People 2021: Navigating Uncertainty" (Winona, MN: Springtide Research Institute).
9. Religions for Peace, "1st Assembly on Women, Faith, and Diplomacy."
10. The toolkit comprises an eight-module facilitator guide, participant workbook, and two PowerPoint presentations. It is available, among other resources, at Search for Common Ground's website.
11. United States Institute of Peace.

12 Mounstephen, "Bishop of Truro's Independent Review."
13 Asilbekova and Jailobaeva, "Promoting Religious Freedom."
14 Office of International Religious Freedom, "2020 Report on International Religious Freedom: Kyrgyz Republic" (United States Department of State, May 12, 2021).
15 "Al Minbar-Habima," Facebook.
16 Iftar is the meal that ends the daily Ramadan fast.
17 Meital Bonchek (@meitalbonchek), "I participated today," Twitter, December 14, 2021, 3:17 p.m.; translated from the original Hebrew by the author.
18 Alon Goshen-Gottstein, "Conclusion: Appreciating Interreligious Heroes," 398.

REFERENCES

Religions for Peace. "1st Assembly on Women, Faith, and Diplomacy," last updated November 9, 2020. https://www.rfp.org/women-faith-diplomacy/.

Universal Code of Conduct on Holy Sites. "About the Code." Accessed August 29, 2022. https://www.codeonholysites.org/about-the-code.

"Al Minbar-Habima." Facebook. Accessed August 29, 2022. https://www.facebook.com/alminbarhabima.

Asilbekova, Gulnara, and Kanykey Jailobaeva. "Promoting Religious Freedom Through Government and Civil Society Collaboration in the Kyrgyz Republic." Bishkek: Search for Common Ground Kyrgyzstan, July 2017. https://www.sfcg.org/wp-content/uploads/2017/08/FoR-in-Kyrgyzstan-Final_Evaluation_Report_04.08.2017-1-2.pdf.

Baumann, Jonas, Daniel Finnbogason, and Isak Svensson. "Rethinking Mediation: Resolving Religious Conflicts." *CSS Policy Perspectives* 6, no. 1 (February 2018): 1–4. https://css.ethz.ch/en/publications/csspolicyperspectives/details.html?id=/r/e/t/h/rethinking_mediation_resolving_religious.

Bonchek, Meital (@meitalbonchek). "I participated today in a festive event at the British Ambassador's residence." Twitter, December 14, 2021, 3:17 p.m. https://twitter.com/meitalbonchek/status/1470865620333961223?t=85TO_NUZfFFrEdN6oMa7Bw&s=19.

Religions for Peace. "Conference of the World Council of Religious Leaders on Faith and Diplomacy: Generations in Dialogue Event Summary," October 16, 2021. https://www.rfp.org/conference-of-the-world-council-of-religious-leaders-on-faith-and-diplomacy-generations-in-dialogue-event-summary/.

Francis. *Fratelli Tutti* [Encyclical Letter on Fraternity and Social Friendship]. October 3, 2020. https://www.vatican.va/content/francesco/en/encyclicals/documents/papafrancesco_20201003_enciclica-fratelli-tutti.html.

Goshen-Gottstein, Alon. "Conclusion: Appreciating Interreligious Heroes." In *Interreligious Heroes: Role Models and Spiritual Exemplars for Interfaith Practice*, edited by Alon Goshen-Gottstein, 397–406. Eugene, OR: Wipf & Stock, 2021.

Hackett, Conrad, and Brian J. Grim, et al. "The Global Religious Landscape." Washington, DC: Pew Research Center, December 18, 2012. https://www.pewresearch.org/religion/2012/12/18/global-religious-landscape-about/.

Institute for Economics & Peace. "Five Key Questions Answered on the Link Between Peace and Religion: A Global Statistical Analysis on the Empirical Link Between Peace and Religion," October 2014. https://www.economicsandpeace.org/wp-content/uploads/2015/06/Peace-and-Religion-Report.pdf.

Mounstephen, Philip. "Bishop of Truro's Independent Review for the Foreign Secretary of FCO Support for Persecuted Christians: Final Report and Recommendations." London: Foreign & Commonwealth Office, July 4, 2019. https://christianpersecutionreview.org.uk/report/.

Office of International Religious Freedom. "2020 Report on International Religious Freedom: Kyrgyz Republic." United States Department of State, May 12, 2021. https://www.state.gov/reports/2020-report-on-international-religious-freedom/kyrgyzstan/.

Search for Common Ground. "The Common Ground Approach to Religious Engagement," September 25, 2020. https://www.sfcg.org/the-common-ground-approach-to-religious-engagement/.

"The State of Religion & Young People 2021: Navigating Uncertainty." Winona, MN: Springtide Research Institute, 2021. https://www.springtideresearch.org/research/the-state-of-religion-2021.

United Nations Alliance of Civilizations. "The United Nations Plan of Action to Safeguard Religious Sites: In Unity and Solidarity for Safe and Peaceful Worship," September 12, 2019. https://forsafeworship.org/plan-of-action/.

United States Institute of Peace. "Religious Engagement in Peacebuilding - A Common Ground Approach." Accessed August 29, 2022. https://www.usip.org/academy/catalog/religious-engagement-peacebuilding-common-ground-approach.

MICHAEL DANIEL DRIESSEN

INTERRELIGIOUS ENGAGEMENT AND POLITICAL THEORY
Between Virtue Ethics and Religious Humanism

INTRODUCTION

The last ten years have seen a dramatic growth in interreligious initiatives on the international stage, sometimes in spectacular form. This growth has been felt particularly in the broader Middle East and Mediterranean region, with a series of high-level interreligious initiatives and declarations providing an emphatic counterpoint to religiously-identified conflicts and violence in the region and all the portending fears of a clash of civilizations they seemed to inspire. As this special volume observes, these initiatives can be understood to represent new forms of interreligious diplomacy or, as Fabio Petito and others have argued, new forms of "interreligious engagement."[1] For a scholar of political science, the growth of interreligious diplomacy in the Middle East raises complex and varied questions. Among others: is interreligious diplomacy appropriate or effective as a strategy to achieve conflict resolution or promote international cooperation? What does interreligious diplomacy reveal about the contested nature of religious authority in the region and its relation to politics? How do religious leaders, communities and people view interreligious diplomacy? What does interreligious diplomacy *do* anyway?

On the one hand, interreligious diplomacy could be understood as simply seeking to channel forms of multi-religious collaboration for common humanitarian ends. These initiatives, however, have also supported innovative ways of thinking about the relationship between religion and global politics. Thus, theoretically rich concepts like "inclusive citizenship" and "human fraternity" have been introduced by recent interreligious declarations in the Middle East and Mediterranean region and caught the attention of both religious leaders and international policymakers. In this paper, I consider some of the background sources of political theology that are advanced in these developments and, in particular, the model of religion-state partnership they seem to imply, both at the international and domestic level of politics. Contemporary interreligious engagement strategies, especially in the broader Mediterranean region, have emphasized the roles of religious communities in creating both common forms of public morality and social solidarity. In doing so, I argue, they can be understood to draw on or reflect the political traditions of both "virtue ethics" and "religious humanism." These two traditions are distinct and sometimes in tension with each other. Articulating the influence of these two traditions on contemporary forms of interreligious engagement can help to illustrate 1) the multiple audiences they attract (including both conservative and liberal religious and political actors); 2) the unresolved political and religious dilemmas they bring forward; and 3) the opportunities and risks they pose for guiding future political development in the region.

The essay is organized as follows. It begins by considering the tradition of religious humanism. In order to do so, it draws a line from the influence of religious humanism on postwar Christian democratic attempts to promote reconciliation and political stability in Europe to parallel efforts in the Middle East today. The second half of the essay then turns to the tradition of virtue ethics and considers the ways in which contemporary interreligious projects in the region are advancing important arguments about the role of religion in public life and critiquing international norms and practices in doing so. While recognizing the risks inherent in these projects, especially with respect to the dynamics of state power, the essay argues that when combined and balanced they provide an innovative roadmap for public religious engagement and multi-religious collaboration for peace in the broader Mediterranean region.

INTERRELIGIOUS DIALOGUE AND RELIGIOUS HUMANISM

This section begins with a brief consideration of the tradition of Christian humanism and its influence on a series of post-war initiatives for reconciliation and reconstruction in Europe. It then applies a similar lens to understand the political content of interreligious efforts in the broader Middle East today.

Christian—or what Jacques Maritain defined as "integral"—humanism represented an important effort to develop a Christian approach to political modernity that could provide a compelling political vision in favor of individual rights, social justice, and freedom while remaining in the service of Christian truth claims and the theological tradition of the Catholic Church.[2]

One of the central features of Christian humanism is the way in which it sought to overcome a question about the form of the state and the nature of political authority in relation to religion in modernity. This question had been at the heart of decades of conflict between the forces of church and state in Europe and was not peripheral to the thirty years of intense global violence and national hostilities that marked the First and Second World Wars. Throughout these years of conflict, the Catholic Church (in particular) as well as other Christian denominations assumed ambiguous positions about the authoritarian power of corporate, religiously-identified states in Europe. Maritain's conceptualization of integral humanism, in fact, could be understood as the antithesis of the authoritarian, nationalist conceptualization of integralism that had facilitated Catholic support for corporatist and fascist regimes across the continent. In part, it was the violence of the World Wars, which broadly pitted liberal and authoritarian states in Europe against each other, that pushed forward the development of Christian humanism and its eventual triumph as a guiding model for postwar Catholic and Christian political action.

One of the keys of Christian humanism in this sense is that it adopted a non-antagonistic understanding of the ideal relationship between religion, state, and society within a democratic political regime. In doing so it rejected an authoritarian model of the state, whether in its clerical-fascist or traditional-monarchic mode. At the same time, it rejected a hard, liberal, secular model of the state that equated modernization with an aggressive promotion of secularization and the rigid differentiation of social, political, and religious spheres. Instead, Christian humanism championed a model of religion and state in which religious forces—including the entire religious lifeworld of religious institutions, civic associations, worker collectives, public intellectuals, parishes, and citizens—were mobilized as co-creators of an open model of civil society. In this model, religious forces worked to foster and sustain a shared moral political background that prized social cooperation for the common good within a society defined by pluralism and freedom.

By emphasizing the religious responsibilities that individual citizens have towards each other, this vision of politics as one of co-authorship required what might be described as a greater democratic concern for "the other." As Pope Paul VI wrote in his 1964 encyclical *Ecclesiam Suam*,

But it seems to Us that the sort of relationship for the Church to establish with the world should be more in the nature of a dialogue . . . this method of approach is demanded nowadays by the prevalent understanding of the relationship between the sacred and the profane. It is demanded by the dynamic course of action which is changing the face of modern society. It is demanded by the pluralism of society, and by the maturity man has reached in this day and age. Be he religious or not, his secular education has enabled him to think and speak, and conduct a dialogue with dignity.

Moreover, the very fact that he engages in a dialogue of this sort is proof of his consideration and esteem for others, his understanding and his kindness . . . if, in our desire to respect a man's freedom and dignity, his conversion to the true faith is not the immediate object of our dialogue with him, we nevertheless try to help him and to dispose him for a fuller sharing of ideas and convictions.[3]

By championing these ideals of co-authorship and social responsibility from within the Christian tradition itself, Christian humanism helped unlock the public capacities of religious forces and religious thinking at the time. Critically, it allowed them to no longer assume a defensive posture in their role in politics. This change of posture was further aided by the religion-state arrangements struck by a number of postwar European states, including Italy and Germany, who constitutionally recognized and assured the public contribution of religion to the democratic life of their nations. In important ways, this acknowledgement helped to restore confidence in religion's place within society, directing Christian-inspired actors and movements to pour their public energies into civic, democratic action in solidarity with others. The political vision of Christian humanism, in other words, gave postwar European religious forces a strong foot to stand on as participants in the reconstruction of European politics and society. Forlenza and Thomassen have recently explored this dynamism as deriving from what they describe as the political spirituality of the Christian democratic movement.[4] The driving motivation of early Christian democratizers in Europe, they argue, as well as their success in mobilizing large segments of their societies, simply cannot be understood in terms of rational self-interest or otherwise. The full political weight and influence of Christian democracy in Europe can only be fully appreciated by recognizing its wider religious and spiritual appeal.

In particular, these ideas became the blueprint for a trio of Christian democratic statesmen, namely Robert Schumann, Konrad Adenauer, and Alcide de Gasperi, from France, Germany, and Italy, respectively, who became founding figures in the establishment of the European Union. In their vision for Europe, political and social reconciliation—between European nations and within European societies—was made possible within a framework of mutual political responsibility among a plurality of religious and social forces.

Giving this model a name was important in the European experience. "Christian humanism" and "Christian democracy," which find strong resonance in the concepts of human fraternity and inclusive citizenship, came to represent an ideal of religious-public partnership that guided the construction of EU institutions, the making of European constitutions, national legislation on welfare, and the defense of human rights and political freedoms.

It is worth emphasizing that this development represented a major religious reckoning for Christianity, one that was pushed forward and challenged by the violence and horrors of World War II and the ambiguous posture of Christians vis-à-vis that violence. In other words, it grew out of a moment of civilizational crisis within European politics and within European Christianity that created the opportunity and need for a re-organization of religion's place in society and politics.

It is also worth noting that this model of Christian democracy has lost its vigor in Europe today, for a number of reasons,[5] and that the rise or return of a more aggressive Christian nationalism is in part the result. Without a model for mobilizing the faithful towards meaningful public engagement, and without dialogue on the basis of those terms with broader European society, older religious-political options have resurfaced. Apologetic thinking about more authoritarian forms of nationalism have returned across the continent and elsewhere around the world. In important ways, these developments reveal a European Christianity that is once again unsure about its public role and capacities.[6]

DIALOGUE AND RELIGIOUS HUMANISM IN THE MEDITERRANEAN

This short sketch of Christian humanism in postwar Europe puts recent dialogue efforts in the broader Middle East into revealing angles of relief. Among other things, it helps expose a parallel ferment around a similar constellation of ideas in the region today. In the face of a deep political and religious crisis, religious leaders and communities, often within the framework of multi-faith initiatives, have increasingly gravitated towards ideas of citizenship and interreligious solidarity. As they have struggled to respond to questions of social fragmentation, religious pluralism, the rights of religious others, the aspirations of the Arab Spring, the violence of the Islamic State, or the wars in Syria, Yemen, and Libya, a growing religious conviction has been expressed that the ideals of citizenship, religious social responsibility, and human solidarity represent the best way forward to build a durable peace in the region.

One element propelling this interest in inclusive citizenship forward has been the evolving response of religious communities to violence against religious minorities in the region and their engagement on the question of religious freedom. The 2016 Marrakesh Declaration, for example, drew on classical principles of Islamic jurisprudence to make a strong claim that non-Muslim religious minorities deserve the same protections of dignity, rights, and freedoms as Muslim majorities in the region. The Declaration ended with an appeal to "develop a jurisprudence of the concept of 'citizenship' which is inclusive of diverse groups," in order to overcome the state of conflict and crisis in the region. This increasing attention to political rights and participation was also pushed forward by the events of the Arab Spring, as can be seen in the 2011 and 2017 al-Azhar Declarations on freedom and citizenship. Both documents, issued by the highest officials of Islam in Egypt, recognized the legitimacy of the Egyptian and Arab peoples' aspirations for democracy and used religious language to support the strengthening of citizenship in the region. The 2019 Human Fraternity document, signed by Pope Francis and the grand imam of al-Azhar, Sheikh Ahmed al-Tayeb, continued this development and declared that,

> The concept of citizenship is based on the equality of rights and duties, under which all enjoy justice. It is therefore crucial to establish in our societies the concept of full citizenship and reject the discriminatory use of the term minorities which engenders feelings of isolation and inferiority.[7]

In some ways, it is striking to see how the strengthening of citizen rights and support for citizenship formation has been embraced in the region and proposed as a solution to both religious and political crises. As was the case in the aftermath of World War II, this support seems to reflect a conviction that in order to be transformative, interreligious dialogue efforts must extend beyond simply condemning religious violence in the name of Islam (or Christianity), as many religious leaders have done. Rather, it must involve long-run efforts of political, intellectual, and social development and offer a compelling and integral vision of how to do so. In this sense, the call for "comprehensive" or "inclusive" citizenship found in recent interreligious declarations could be seen to both reaffirm basic commitments to citizen rights and liberties, but also to seek the long-term participation and integration of various religious and social "others" in public life.[8]

Recent appeals to human fraternity in interreligious declarations in the region and beyond capture this vision in a particular way and reveal its indebtedness to the longer tradition of religious humanism. The 2019 Document on Human Fraternity, for example, explicitly connects "full citizenship" to a "human fraternity" that "embraces all human beings, unites them and renders them equal."[9] For Pope Francis, who has repeatedly invoked and championed the concept throughout his papacy, religious humanism advances individual rights, freedom, and dignity through religiously-inspired forms of social solidarity or "social friendship," as he has defined it.[10]

On this point, the recent campaign in favor of "Humanitarian Islam" (*al-islām lil-insānīyah*) led by Nahdlatul Ulama (NU) in Indonesia, the largest Islamic association in the world, is even more explicit. Through a multi-religious series of manifestos, declarations, and events,[11] NU has attempted to promote the concept of Humanitarian Islam as a source of religious, social, and political renewal in favor of universal rights and a response to what it diagnoses as a civilizational crisis within the Islamic world.[12] In 2019, leaders of the Humanitarian Islam movement worked together with the Centrist Democrat International (the global network of Christian Democratic parties)[13] to adopt a resolution in Rome that bears witness to the centrality of religious humanism in their shared, ongoing efforts to support a faith-inspired human rights agenda,[14] stating,

> We believe that Humanitarian Islam and the diverse strands of humanist philosophy that historically emerged in the West are kindred traditions, whose spiritual and philosophical values are consonant with—and, in the case of Western humanism, helped to shape and secure the adoption of—the Universal Declaration of Human Rights (UDHR) . . . It is our belief that the spirit of universal human

fraternity that animates UDHR, Christian humanism and the global Humanitarian Islam movement represents a compelling moral, ethical, religious and, indeed, political basis for close cooperation between CDI member parties, and between people of goodwill of every faith and nation.[15]

Like the Marrakesh and al-Azhar Declarations, the Humanitarian Islam movement promotes a rights-based model of political development that calls on religious actors to lead efforts in support of civic participation and social solidarity. In doing so, these initiatives construct an alternative religious-political discourse in the region and create new opportunities for religious communities in the process.

INTERRELIGIOUS DIALOGUE AND VIRTUE ETHICS

So far, I have relied on the tradition of religious humanism to emphasize some of the ways that recent dialogue initiatives have advanced a more confidently rights-centered model of public religious engagement in the region. In doing so, the initiatives can be seen to positively ring with central elements of the liberal, international political agenda in favor of human rights, democracy, and pluralism. From this angle, as I argue elsewhere,[16] the global rise of interreligious dialogue activity might be interpreted as part of the ongoing development of religion in modernity—a complex process through which religious communities seek to adapt to, negotiate with, reconcile themselves to, and positively claim modernity from within the specific religious logic of their traditions. The very nature of interreligious dialogue facilitates this process, helping global religious communities present themselves as at ease with and supportive of progressive gains in the field of rights, inclusivity of others, and attention to the marginalized. It is perhaps for this very reason that powerful, international governmental actors based in the West, including the United Nations, the United States, the European Union and its member states, have invested in interreligious dialogue activities as a diplomatic practice, not simply because they offer ways to manage and address practical issues rising from religious diversity, but also because the vision presented for doing so does not seem to fundamentally threaten liberal norms and hopes. *Fratelli Tutti*, for example, Pope Francis's interreligious dialogue-inspired encyclical on solidarity and social friendship (which directly builds on the Document on Human Fraternity) includes more approving references to the United Nations than to the Holy Spirit.

And yet this characterization of interreligious dialogue as mostly in tune with liberal modernity and its international manifestations is incomplete. In order to appreciate some of the wider religious appeal of interreligious efforts in the region and evaluate some of the claims these initiatives have made, it is helpful to examine them from within the tradition of virtue ethics, especially as developed in the work of Alasdair MacIntyre, but also with respect to political traditions that emphasize the role of religion in producing and maintaining the moral virtues necessary for an active and well-ordered political society.

Tradition and Telos
Scholarship on virtue ethics emphasizes that social coordination in favor of the common good requires widespread habits of cooperation and moral virtue which, like the common good, are not readily apparent or acquired by individuals on the basis of their free capacity to reason alone. Rather, for MacIntyre and others,[17] recognizing and acquiring moral virtue depends on knowing something about the purpose of human beings, their *telos*—what humans were made for and why they exist. The answers to these teleological questions, in turn, are typically provided by tradition and religious narratives that conserve stories about the good over time.[18] For virtue ethics, therefore, a strong concept of the good is necessary to orient the individual rights and freedom provided by a democratic regime towards the construction and preservation of a common political welfare.

As the last section began to observe, key elements of both religious humanism and contemporary discourse on interreligious dialogue in the Middle East include strong teleological claims. Many interreligious declarations, for example, and the statements they make about the necessity of political rights or religious freedom, rest on a theological affirmation of the innate dignity of human beings as divinely ordained by God, whether derived from the *imago dei* of the book of Genesis or as conferred on Adam by God in the Qur'an. In these affirmations, human beings are understood to be divinely created both *with* and *for* dignity. The uncreated origin of human dignity was central in the justification of human rights developed by Christian political philosophers like Maritain and influenced both the drafting of the Universal Declaration of Human Rights and the influential *Dignitatis Humanae* declaration on Religious Freedom at Vatican II.[19] The centrality of divinely conferred dignity is also at the center of the Marrakesh Declaration's insistence on citizenship and religious freedom,[20] as well as in the Document on Human Fraternity, which beings with an invocation:

> In the name of God, who has created all human beings equal in rights, duties and dignity, and who has called them to live together as brothers and sisters, to fill the earth and make known the values of goodness, love and peace.[21]

While the proposition that humans are created with and for equal dignity has long been used as the basis for declaring the universality of human rights, following virtue ethics, the teleological implications of this justification are essential and have consequences for the role of religion in public life. Declaring divinely endowed dignity as the reason for protecting the freedom of individuals and respecting pluralism, for example, can be interpreted as an active defense of religious life as a public good, one that contributes to the creation of a moral community that regenerates and inculcates the dignity proposition and that values freedom and civic solidarity. Important strands of Catholic political philosophy continue to develop this line of thinking on the basis of theories of natural law and draw a line from Aristotle to Aquinas and sometimes to Vatican II to do so.[22]

Similar propositions can be found in some contemporary Islamic scholarship on traditional Islamic jurisprudence (*usul al-fiqh*) that focuses on the higher objectives of the sharia (*maqasid al sharia*).[23] In an essay reflecting on the role of natural law in classic Islamic jurisprudence, for example, Emon describes what he defines as a soft natural law position in medieval Islamic thought, which was also in debt to and in awe of Aristotle.[24] He argues that this philosophical tradition continues to inform global Islamic political reflection, including in its attempt to delimit the extent to which human reason in relation to revelation should serve as an independent source of law and politics in modernity. What emerges, Emon argues, is a middle position on the legitimacy of moral human agency that is more restricted than that elevated by liberalism and which is limited by the higher objectives of Islam (*maqasid al-sharia*) as derived from the Quran. Like other scholars of Islamic studies, rather than Aquinas, Emon traces the line from Aristotle to Ibn Sina/Avicenna and sees its influence at work in al-Ghazali's oft-used five higher objectives of the sharia.[25]

Although it is not a perfect fit, there is a closeness here to MacIntyre's theory of virtue ethics, with the *maqasid* providing the telos—the higher objectives—to which virtues strive and the basis on which reason judges the best interest (*maslaha*) of the common good, and which provides the motivation and the religious moral responsibility to struggle against the self for its achievement.

Recent interreligious declarations have made recourse to similar claims in order to justify a strong account of dignity, minority rights, religious freedom, and pluralism from within their respective religious traditions. In doing so, these declarations also advance virtue ethics' criticism of liberalism's claims to a more radical autonomy of individual agency within the political community, and they appeal to the moral force of religious tradition to guide and limit public reason and its defense of rights. These declarations, in making this appeal, argue that religious traditions serve the pursuit of human rights well. In his searing critique of the modern liberal state, Hallaq's work is expressive in this sense and explicitly draws on MacIntyre to assert the need to recuperate public moral sources—which he looks to in the pre-modern paradigm of sharia—in order to rehumanize political development.[26] As he writes,

> "[T]he relegation of the moral imperative to a secondary status . . . has been at the core of the modern project, leading us to promote or ignore poverty, social disintegration, and the deplorable destruction of the very earth that nourishes humankind, in terms of both material exploitation *and* value. . . . The continuing deep effects of [the classic Muslim] tradition on modern Muslims lends credence to MacIntyre's critique of the Enlightenment concept of autonomous rationality, where ethical values are assumed to issue from noumenal reason."[27]

This criticism of secular liberalism's capacity to regenerate concern for the common good over time sheds a different light on recent interreligious declarations' emphasis on religious renewal. In addition to calling for the long-run development of a stronger concept of citizenship, for example, one of the major stated aims of the Marrakesh Declaration is to

> contribute to the broader legal discourse surrounding contractual citizenship and the protection of minorities, to awaken the dynamism of Muslim societies and encourage the creation a broad-based movement of protecting religious minorities in Muslim lands.[28]

Likewise, the Document on Human Fraternity affirmed

the importance of awakening religious awareness and the need to revive this awareness in the hearts of new generations through sound education and an adherence to moral values and upright religious teachings. In this way we can confront tendencies that are individualistic, selfish, conflicting, and also address radicalism and blind extremism in all its forms and expressions.[29]

The importance of virtue ethics in recent interreligious initiatives, and the place of religious renewal, might be best encapsulated by the Alliance of Virtue project, promoted by Sheikh Abdallah bin Bayyah's Forum for Promoting Peace in Muslim Societies, the same association that organized the 2016 Marrakesh Declaration. The Alliance of Virtue Charter, signed in 2019, highlights the role of religious communities as generators of universal values that help create and sustain the peace and political rights envisioned by international accords like the Universal Declaration of Human Rights. The Alliance of Virtue project includes support from notable Christian, Muslim, and Jewish leaders in the United States and found important echoes among conservative scholars and actors campaigning for religious freedom there.[30] William Vendley, Emeritus Secretary General of Religions for Peace and a member of the Alliance of Virtue steering committee, recently summarized the project and its relationship to human rights in the following terms:

> Our Alliance of Virtue is an utterly essential compliment to one of the great achievements of the modern era. We are a period that is dominated by human rights which is a common language for us. We prospered because of it. But rights alone are not enough. Rights protect, but virtues perfect. Virtue is the domain where we raise the question how can we become a good society. Virtues link becoming a good person with becoming a good society. They are the two legs upon which inclusive citizenship can stand firmly. In modernity we are trying to stand on only one leg, the rights leg. It is not enough.[31]

RISKS AND OPPORTUNITIES

This essay has turned to the traditions of religious humanism and virtue ethics to better understand the emerging political vision expressed in recent interreligious diplomatic efforts in the broader Middle East region. The tradition of religious humanism helps us to consider the ways in which these interreligious efforts have offered an alternative religious discourse on rights, freedom, and pluralism in the region, one that might complement international liberal norms and hopes for human rights. At the same time, the tradition of virtue ethics helps us to clarify the ways in which these same efforts might challenge liberalism and the extent to which they repropose the centrality of religious traditions in the organization of politics and life. In this sense, the passages on "awakening religious awareness" cited above are critical for understanding the new model of public religious engagement being advanced through dialogue initiatives in the region and why it has found traction among traditional and conservative religious actors as well as liberal ones. In these passages, the positive, long-run development of a society based on political rights and civil liberties is understood to be dependent on the existence of a strong, multi-religious moral community of morally driven citizens. In this model, *political* renewal clearly requires *religious* renewal.

The aims of religious humanism certainly overlap with those of virtue ethics, including in the centrality it places on God-gifted dignity and its concern for religious renewal. It is important to recall here that in Maritain's vision of integral humanism, the divine origins of human dignity worked to put the brakes on the power of the state. Maritain locates dignity in the gift of the creator in part to free and protect the individual from the totalizing power of the state which, as he witnessed in the experience of fascism, devoured human beings and robbed them of their freedom, rights, and dignity. The Humanitarian Islam movement likewise presents God's conferral of dignity on human beings as the basis for resisting state tyranny. As the 2018 Nusantara Manifesto states,

> The Humanitarian Islam movement seeks to restore human nature to what Islam regards as its pure and original state (*fiṭrah*)—as symbolized by the act of God breathing life into the Prophet Adam—and to eliminate the widespread practice of using religion to incite hatred and violence towards others ... *Fiṭrah* stands in fundamental opposition to tyranny (*ṭughyān*), which forcibly silences the liberating voice of conscience and subordinates it to the avaricious dictates of power. Just as *fiṭrah* is the negation of *ṭughyān*, so true religion manifested socially is the negation of the domination of others.[32]

In both these versions of religious humanism, rights and freedoms are not a gift of the state nor are they dependent on it; rather, they proceed from a source above and beyond the state. They are innate and intrinsic to human beings as such. Because they subsist independently of the state, this grounding of human rights also provides a basis for religious communities to criticize and resist the state (or, to use a religious term, prophesize against it), especially when the state does not protect human rights or tries to redefine them to match its political interests. One of the political ideals of Christian democracy that flows from this position was and remains the principle of subsidiarity and, concomitantly, a preference for solving political problems by empowering lower levels of civic society organizations and communities where possible. In adopting subsidiarity as a guide to their policymaking, Christian democracy can be understood to have retained some of the pre-modern Catholic skepticism of the modern state, at least in its more condensed, centralized, supremely sovereign form. This does not mean that Christian democratic parties have an innate preference for a weak state but for a state that shares power and is composed of lower (and higher) orders of social cooperation with myriad civic and religious associations. A number of recent criticisms of liberalism from scholars of Islam have likewise highlighted subsidiarity as consonant with a more decentralized model of the state in which sharia-inspired norms provide one moral base among others for political solidarity and cooperation.[33] And the appeal for Humanitarian Islam would seem to be consistent with such a vision.

Some versions of virtue ethics can work well with a vision of subsidiarity and religious-social democratic cooperation. But in emphasizing the role of tradition, social cohesion, and moral action, virtue ethics can also provide grist for other kinds of political regimes. As a number of critics of social capital have noted,[34] the kinds of social capital that virtue ethics sees religious traditions providing are helpful for both democracies and many authoritarian regimes. In her exploration of social capital in the Middle East, Jamal,[35] for example, argues that there is another side to social capital, one that reproduces and strengthens authoritarian norms and practices by emphasizing political virtues such as loyalty, trust, and stability. A number of authors have criticized the Forum for Promoting Peace's projects on similar grounds, arguing that the Forum, and the vision of Abdallah bin Bayyah in particular, has promoted a theology of obedience and social cohesion that serves to strengthen and justify the authoritarian power of the Forum's host country, the United Arab Emirates.[36] Rather than advocate for a passive obedience, however (and whether that is the best way to describe his political thought), it is important to note that Bin Bayyah has promoted a vision of *active* citizen engagement in favor of state and social development in the region. While this does not mean that he directly challenges the authoritarian policies of the UAE, the interreligious efforts of Bin Bayyah and others have partnered with the state on what Masoud has described as a new, "revolutionary," project of modernization in the region which requires higher levels of citizen engagement.[37] Thus, Masoud and others have argued that a number of modernizing Arab regimes, including the UAE, Qatar, Jordan, and Saudi Arabia, have adopted ambitious strategies to remake their societies into a virtuous, hard-working, highly educated, and entrepreneurial team of citizens.[38] As evidence, Masoud cites Saudi Arabia's Vision 2030 program, which states that it seeks to foster "the values of entrepreneurship, generosity, volunteering, excellence, hard work, ambition and optimism," and an official Egyptian appeal for "creative, responsible and competitive" citizens.[39] This vision of active citizenship, solidarity, and social cohesion outlined by recent interreligious declarations—and their appeal for virtuous citizens to earnestly work for the good of society—might well funnel into the modernizing strategies of a number of post-Arab Spring authoritarian regimes seeking stability, development, and good governance.

On this score, a virtue ethics approach to politics appears more ambiguous about the role of the state than does a religious humanism approach. It could be observed, for example, that documents like the Marrakesh Declaration and the Document on Human Fraternity have said little about the actual form of the state or the extent to which it should constitutionally share power with its citizens. Tellingly, while strongly advocating for the concept of full or inclusive citizenship, both documents studiously avoid mention of the word "democracy." These declarations, in particular,[40] are clearly ambivalent about the role and form of the state, and the avenues of participation and decision-making that it should guarantee to its citizens. In some ways, therefore, the virtue ethics approach embedded in interreligious declarations could also be seen to challenge international assumptions about the sources and ends of cooperation and rights.

This ambivalence is not necessarily debilitating. Virtue ethics is certainly not inimical to democracy *per se* and, as alluded to above, much recent work in this tradition expressly understands itself as participating in a broader effort to re-establish healthy patterns of democratic cooperation in the United States and elsewhere. And, while raising important concerns, critics who dismiss recent interreligious initiatives in the Middle East outright on account of their association with regimes like the UAE, Qatar, or Saudi Arabia often miss the substantive growth of ideas and practices expressed within them. They have also often undervalued the extent to which these declarations have facilitated broader efforts by religious traditions to come to terms with late modernity in ways that preserve a strong religious account of society and politics, while also promoting human rights and freedoms.[41]

A CONCLUDING HOPE

As a way of concluding, I would like to suggest that the differences between the religious humanism and virtue ethics approaches might be understood as creating productive tensions within an emerging interreligious framework for political development in the region. When balanced and taken together, the ideals of religious humanism and virtue ethics offer a roadmap for religious actors to take rights, pluralism, and moral community seriously. The potential of this model can be seen especially in the way in which it identifies new opportunities for religious actors and communities to mobilize for a positive vision of politics and act as protagonists of citizenship formation. Like post-war European efforts at reconciliation, interreligious efforts in the region have provided an orienting philosophy and a platform for constructive religious-political engagement in favor of peace and pluralism. This substantive—as opposed to simply aggregate—growth of dialogue efforts in the Middle East over the last two decades is promising and represents a historical development in the region. The strengthening of interreligious engagement projects in the region, therefore, as seen through thickening proposals of citizenship and human solidarity, represents a welcome attempt to construct a religiously meaningful and politically balanced approach to public religious engagement. And as such, it offers a realistic and hopeful vision of political development for the Middle East and beyond.

NOTES

1 Petito, Daou and Driessen, *Human Fraternity and Inclusive Citizenship*.
2 Maritain, "Integral Humanism."
3 Paul IV, *Ecclesiam Suam*.
4 Forlenza and Thomassen, *Italian Christian Democracy*. It is worth noting here that Maritain's conceptualization of integral humanism was not the only influence directing the construction of Christian democratic parties' political ideology and action at the time. Maritain, in fact, distanced himself from Christian democratic parties despite his outsized influence on them, and important debates about the relationship between Maritain and Christian

democratic principles remain relevant in the scholarship today. See, for example, Diotallevi, "Catholic Liberal Dream?" Nevertheless, integral humanism serves as a reasonable proxy—at least in this essay—for a number of the ideals that inspired the Christian democratic movement.

5 For some discussion see Taylor, "Catholic Cosmopolitanism and the Future of Human Rights."

6 In this sense, as I argue elsewhere, the contemporary political circumstances of Europe represent a propitious time to revisit the tradition of religious humanism and Christian democracy. See Driessen, "Catholicism and European Politics: Introducing Contemporary Dynamics."

7 "Document on 'Human Fraternity for World Peace and Living Together' Signed by His Holiness Pope Francis and the Grand Imam of Al-Azhar Ahamad al-Tayyib (Abu Dhabi, 4 February 2019)."

8 Petito Petito, Daou and Driessen, *Human Fraternity and Inclusive Citizenship*.

9 As the opening reference to Human Fraternity in the document describes it. Cardinal Pietro Parolin, Pope Francis's Secretary of State, has recently made the intent to connect citizenship with fraternity in the document clear. See Parolin, "Essere Mediterranei: Fratelli e Cittadini Del «Mare Nostro»."

10 Driessen, "Catholicism and European Politics."

11 In particular through the 2016 International Summit of Moderate Islamic Leaders (ISOMIL) Nahdlatul Ulema Declaration, the 2017 Gerakan Penuda Ansor Declaration on Humanitarian Islam and the 2018 Nusantra Manifesto.

12 A crisis which it identifies with a closed, revolutionary form of political Islam. See, especially, the 2017 Gerakan Pemuda Ansor Declaration on Humanitarian Islam. As the Ansor Declaration claims, "The Islamic world is in the midst of a rapidly metastasizing crisis, with no apparent sign of remission."

13 The Centrist Democrat International (CDI) is an international network of Christian democratic parties and was formerly named the Christian Democratic International. The organization still defines its purpose as supporting "Christian democracy, integral humanism and interreligious dialogue," which is the tagline it uses to describe its activities on its official homepage.

14 "Resolution on Ethics and Values That Should Guide the Exercise of Power." In 2019, the Indonesian Nationalist Awakening Party (PKB), which is historically associated with NU, became a formal member of CDI. H. Anggia Ermarini, the party's deputy general-secretary and also then-chairperson of the NU's young adult women's movement (or *Fatayat*, which has an estimated of 7 million members), presented the resolution for adoption at the meeting in Rome.

15 The resolution begins with the following: "Recognizing that the spiritual, philosophical and historical origins of the Centrist Democrat International (CDI) lie in the traditions of Christian humanism, and the response of Christian Democratic political movements to the profound moral and geopolitical crisis that European and Latin American nations faced after World War II. . . . [and] Acknowledging the central role of the humanist tradition, and of Christian

Democratic political movements which helped inspire and secure the adoption of the Universal Declaration of Human Rights." The NU also presented a resolution earlier in the same year (2019) which was adopted by the CDI and that formally endorsed the Document on Human Fraternity and noted its resonance with Humanitarian Islam.

16 Driessen, *The Global Politics of Interreligious Dialogue: Religious Change, Citizenship and Solidarity in the Middle East*.
17 See, especially, MacIntyre, *After Virtue: A Study in Moral Theory*.
18 See Murphy, Kallenberg, and Nation, eds., *Virtues and Practices in the Christian Tradition: Christian Ethics after MacIntyre* and Thomas, "Building Communities of Character: Foreign Aid Policy and Faith-Based Organizations."
19 See Moyn, *Christian Human Rights*.
20 Following its preface, the unabridged Marrakesh Declaration begins by declaring in point 1 that "God bestowed dignity on all human beings regardless of their race, color, language or belief," and then directly moves to point 2, namely, that "This dignity requires that human beings must be granted freedom of choice." It should be noted that the Alliance of Virtue, also sponsored by the Forum for Promoting Peace in Muslim Societies, makes a similar argument and cites *Dignitatis Humanae* in doing so.
21 "Document on Human Fraternity."
22 The above cited *Dignitatis Humanae*, for example, which altered the path of traditional Catholic positions on democracy and religious freedom, simultaneously states that (3) "Government therefore ought indeed to take account of the religious life of the citizenry and show it favor, since the function of government is to make provision for the common welfare," and (6) "Government is also to help create conditions favorable to the fostering of religious life, in order that the people may be truly enabled to exercise their religious rights and to fulfill their religious duties, and also in order that society itself may profit by the moral qualities of justice and peace which have their origin in men's faithfulness to God and to His holy will."
23 See, among others, Duderija, ed., *Maqasid Al-Shari'a and Contemporary Reformist Muslim Thought: An Examination*; Auda, *Maqasid al-Shariah as Philosophy of Islamic Law: A Systems Approach*; and Emon, "Islam Natural Law Theories."
24 Emon, "Islam Natural Law Theories."
25 Emon reads al Ghazail as still writing "in the shadow of classical Greek philosophy" which al Ghazali came to through Ibn Sina (Avicenna), whom, however, al Ghazli also famously critiqued in his work *The Incoherence of the Philosophers*. For another account of the Islamic appeal to natural law in recent interreligious dialogue efforts, see Diez, "The Alliance of Virtue: Towards an Islamic Natural Law?"
26 Hallaq, *The Impossible State: Islam, Politics, and Modernity's Moral Predicament*.
27 Hallaq, *The Impossible State*, 4–5. He then goes on to quote MacIntyre on the same page, writing, "Rational enquiry and thus ethical values are embedded,

MacIntyre rightly observes, 'in a *tradition, a conception* according to which the standards of rational justification themselves emerge from and are part of a history in which they are vindicated" and then states a few pages later that, "The Shari'a. . . . represented and was constituted by a moral law, hence its significance to us as a moral resource for the modern project (equivalent to Aristotle and Aquinas in the MacIntyrean proposal)" (Hallaq, *Impossible State*, 5, 10).

28 Marrakesh Declaration, "About." This was originally stated in the concept note for the conference and is repeated on the home page of the Declaration's official website.

29 "Document on Human Fraternity." This language was then recapitulated in Pope Francis's *Fratelli Tutti* encyclical as follows, "among the most important causes of the crises of the modern world are a desensitized human conscience, a distancing from religious values and the prevailing individualism accompanied by materialistic philosophies that deify the human person and introduce worldly and material values in place of supreme and transcendental principles."

30 Sam Brownback, then the U.S. Ambassador for Religious Freedom abroad, for example, participated in both an earlier iteration of the Alliance of Virtue pact in 2018 and than again at the 2019 launch. Hamza Yusuf, who spearheaded much of the Alliance of Virtue efforts was an important presence at the U.S.-sponsored ministerials on Religious Freedom in 2018 and 2019 and was appointed by then-U.S. Secretary of State Mike Pompeo to the Commission on Unalienable Rights, chaired by prominent conservative scholar Mary Ann Glendon and charged with reviewing the role of human rights in American public policy. Yusuf is also a lead participant in the Religious Freedom Institute's Virtues Project, which "explores ways that classical traditions of virtue, rooted in the transcendent, might serve as a potent antidote to the plummeting consensus in America on what it means to pursue the common good." The Religious Freedom Institute also participated in the drafting of the Alliance of Virtue Charter.

31 Vendley, "Untitled." These remarks were delivered at the Eighth Assembly of the Abu Dhabi Forum for Peace, which was organized by the Forum for Promoting Peace in Muslim Societies and titled "Inclusive Citizenship: From Mutual Coexistence to Shared Conscience" on December 5, 2021.

32 "Nusantara Manifesto."

33 See, for example, Winter, "In Search of a Contemporary Sharī'a Discourse of Pluralism."

34 See Berman, "Civil Society and the Collapse of the Weimar Republic"; and Jamal, "When Is Social Trust a Desirable Outcome?: Examining Levels of Trust in the Arab World."

35 Jamal, "When is Social Trust a Desirable Outcome?"

36 Warren, *Rivals in the Gulf: Yusuf al-Qaradawi, Abdullah Bin Bayyah, and the Qatar-UAE Contest over the Arab Spring and the Gulf Crisis* and Quisay and

Parker, "On the Theology of Obedience: An Analysis of Shaykh Bin Bayyah and Shaykh Hamza Yusuf's Political Thought."

37 Masoud, "The Arab Spring at 10: Kings or People?," 146.
38 Masoud, "The Arab Spring at 10." See also Jones, *Bedouins into Bourgeois: Remaking Citizens for Globalization*.
39 Masoud, "The Arab Spring at 10," 147.
40 Both the Humanitarian Islam documents, however, as well as the Al-Azhar Declarations and Pope Francis' *Fratelli Tutti* encyclical, are more explicit about their preference for democracy.
41 Driessen, *Global Politics of Interreligious Dialogue*.

REFERENCES

Marrakesh Declaration. "About." Accessed August 31, 2022. https://www.marrakeshdeclaration.org/about/index.html.

Auda, Jasser. *Maqasid al-Shariah as Philosophy of Islamic Law: A Systems Approach*. Herndon, VA: International Institute of Islamic Thought, 2008.

Berman, Sheri. "Civil Society and the Collapse of the Weimar Republic." *World Politics* 49, no. 3 (April 1997): 401–29. https://doi.org/10.1353/wp.1997.0008.

Diez, Martino. "The Alliance of Virtue: Towards an Islamic Natural Law?" Oasis International Foundation, March 30, 2020. https://www.oasiscenter.eu/en/emirates-chart-new-alliance-of-virtue.

"Document on 'Human Fraternity for World Peace and Living Together' Signed by His Holiness Pope Francis and the Grand Imam of Al-Azhar Ahamad al-Tayyib (Abu Dhabi, 4 February 2019)." The Holy See, February 4, 2019. https://www.vatican.va/content/francesco/en/travels/2019/outside/documents/papa-francesco_20190204_documento-fratellanza-umana.html.

Diotallevi, Luca. "1967/1969: The End, or (Just) a Pause of the Catholic Liberal Dream?" *Religions* 11, no. 11 (November 2020). https://doi.org/10.3390/rel11110623.

Driessen, Michael Daniel. *The Global Politics of Interreligious Dialogue: Religious Change, Citizenship and Solidarity in the Middle East*. New York: Oxford University Press, forthcoming.

———. "Catholicism and European Politics: Introducing Contemporary Dynamics." *Religions* 12, no. 4 (April 13, 2021). https://doi.org/10.3390/rel12040271.

Duderija, Adis, ed. *Maqasid Al-Shari'a and Contemporary Reformist Muslim Thought: An Examination*. New York: Palgrave Macmillan, 2014.

Emon, Anver M. "Islam Natural Law Theories." In *Natural Law: A Jewish, Christian, and Islamic Trialogue*, by Anver M. Emon, Matthew Levering, and David Novak, 144–87. Oxford: Oxford University Press, 2014.

Forlenza, Rosario, and Bjorn Thomassen. *Italy's Christian Democracy*. Oxford: Oxford University Press, forthcoming.

Francis. *Fratelli Tutti* [Encyclical Letter on Fraternity and Social Friendship]. October 3, 2020. https://www.vatican.va/content/francesco/en/encyclicals/documents/papa-francesco_20201003_enciclica-fratelli-tutti.html.

"Gerakan Pemuda Ansor Declaration on Humanitarian Islam." Gerakan Pemuda Ansor, May 2017. https://www.baytarrahmah.org/media/2017/Gerakan-Pemuda-Ansor_Declaration-on-Humanitarian-Islam.pdf.

Hallaq, Wael B. *The Impossible State: Islam, Politics, and Modernity's Moral Predicament*. New York: Columbia University Press, 2013.

IDC-CDI. "Homepage." Centrist Democrat International. Accessed August 31, 2022. https://www.idc-cdi.com/.

Jamal, Amaney. "When Is Social Trust a Desirable Outcome?: Examining Levels of Trust in the Arab World." *Comparative Political Studies* 40, no. 11 (November 2007): 1328–49. https://doi.org/10.1177/0010414006291833.

Jones, Calvert W. *Bedouins into Bourgeois: Remaking Citizens for Globalization*. Cambridge: Cambridge University Press, 2017.

MacIntyre, Alasdair C. *After Virtue: A Study in Moral Theory*. Notre Dame, IN: University of Notre Dame Press, 1981.

Maritain, Jacques. "Integral Humanism." In *Integral Humanism, Freedom in the Modern World, and A Letter on Independence*, edited by Otto A. Bird, translated by Otto A. Bird, Joseph Evans, and Richard O'Sullivan. The Collected Works of Jacques Maritain 11. Notre Dame, IN: University of Notre Dame Press, 1996 [1936].

Marrakesh Declaration. "Marrakesh Declaration," January 27, 2016. https://www.marrakeshdeclaration.org/declaration/index.html.

Masoud, Tarek. "The Arab Spring at 10: Kings or People?" *Journal of Democracy* 32, no. 1 (2021): 139–54. https://doi.org/10.1353/jod.2021.0006.

Moyn, Samuel. *Christian Human Rights*. Intellectual History of the Modern Age. Philadelphia: University of Pennsylvania Press, 2015.

Murphy, Nancey C., Brad J. Kallenberg, and Mark Nation, eds. *Virtues and Practices in the Christian Tradition: Christian Ethics after MacIntyre*. Harrisburg, PA: Trinity Press International, 1997.

National Awakening Party. "Resolution on Ethics and Values That Should Guide the Exercise of Power," October 11, 2019. https://www.baytarrahmah.org/media/2019/CDI_Resolution-on-ethics-and-values-that-should-guide-the-exercise-of-power.pdf.

Parolin, Pietro. "Essere Mediterranei: Fratelli e Cittadini Del «Mare Nostro»." [Being Mediterranean: Brothers and Citizens in "Our Sea."] *La Civiltà Cattolica* 1, no. 4072 (February 2020): 368–80. https://www.laciviltacattolica.it/articolo/essere-mediterranei-il-discorso-del-card-parolin/.

Paul VI. *Dignitatis Humanae* [Declaration on Religious Freedom on the Right of the Person and of Communities to Social and Civil Freedom in Matters Religious]. December 7, 1965. https://www.vatican.va/archive/hist_councils/ii_vatican_council/documents/vat-ii_decl_19651207_dignitatis-humanae_en.html.

---. *Ecclesiam Suam* [Encyclical of Pope Paul VI of the Church]. August 6, 1964. https://www.vatican.va/content/paul-vi/en/encyclicals/documents/hf_p-vi_enc_06081964_ecclesiam.html.

Petito, Fabio, Fadi Daou, and Michael D. Driessen, eds. Human Fraternity and Inclusive Citizenship: Interreligious Engagement in the Mediterranean. Milan: Italian Institute for International Political Studies/Ledizioni, 2021. https://www.ispionline.it/en/pubblicazione/human-fraternity-and-inclusive-citizenship-interreligious-engagement-mediterranean-30794.

Quisay, Walaa, and Thomas Parker. "On the Theology of Obedience: An Analysis of Shaykh Bin Bayyah and Shaykh Hamza Yusuf's Political Thought." Maydan: Islamic Thought. AbuSulayman Center for Global Islamic Studies at George Mason University, January 8, 2019. https://themaydan.com/2019/01/theology-obedience-analysis-shaykh-bin-bayyah-shaykh-hamza-yusufs-political-thought/.

Taylor, Leonard. "Catholic Cosmopolitanism and the Future of Human Rights." *Religions* 11, no. 11 (November 2020). https://doi.org/10.3390/rel11110566.

"The Nusantara Manifesto: Adopted and Promulgated by Gerakan Pemuda Ansor and Bayt ar-Rahmah in Yogyakarta, Indonesia on October 25, 2018," October 25, 2018. https://www.baytarrahmah.org/media/2018/Nusantara-Manifesto.pdf.

Thomas, Scott. "Building Communities of Character: Foreign Aid Policy and Faith-Based Organizations." *SAIS Review of International Affairs* 24, no. 2 (2004): 133–48. https://doi.org/10.1353/sais.2004.0045.

Religious Freedom Institute. "Virtues Project: Rediscovering the Meaning of Virtue and the Common Good in Judaism, Christianity, and Islam." Accessed August 31, 2022. https://religiousfreedominstitute.org/virtues-project-2/.

Vendley, William. "Untitled." Remarks delivered at the Eighth Assembly of the Abu Dhabi Forum for Peace, Inclusive Citizenship: From Mutual Coexistence to Shared Conscience, Abu Dhabi, December 5, 2021. https://www.youtube.com/watch?v=6Cn1ljVdVPc.

Warren, David H. *Rivals in the Gulf: Yusuf al-Qaradawi, Abdullah Bin Bayyah, and the Qatar-UAE Contest over the Arab Spring and the Gulf Crisis*. Islam in the World. London: Routledge, 2021.

Winter, Tim. "In Search of a Contemporary Sharī'a Discourse of Pluralism." In *EuARe Lectures: Annual Conference 2019*, edited by Jocelyne Cesari. Bologna: Fondazione per le scienze religiose Giovanni XXIII, 2020.

ABHAY K.

DIPLOMACY

After T.S. Eliot

I
We are the angry men
We are the confused men
Confronting each other
Our heads filled with anger.
When we shout at each other
Our voices are loud and meaningless
As screeching fighter jets
In a war zone

Anger has no shape, anger has no colour,
Anger is a misguided force, a violent emotion;

Those who have trespassed
With full knowledge, to the anger's underworld
Can't remember anything at all – are lost
Forever in the serpentine labyrinth
Of anger, those angry men
Those confused men.

II
Dare not meet their eyes
In anger's underworld,

They are everywhere
Here, there, the eyes are everywhere
Like burning ember in the cold, dark nights
There is a dog howling
And their anger
Is shooting up
And up
Like a gathering storm.

Let them go deeper
In the underworld
Let them go naked
Wearing nothing
Without their masks
In the ring
As true wrestlers
No less –
For the final knockdown
In the dark underworld

III
This is the doomed land
This is the nuked land
Here only heaps of bones
Are left – charred, scattered
Vapourized, melted
Under the cold glow of the moon

It is exactly like this
In anger's dark underworld
Walking alone
Wearing anti-radiation suit

Through mountains of bones
Without uttering a word
Without shedding a drop of tear.

IV
Once, these eyes could see
Not anymore
In this valley of tears
In this valley of doom and death
The lost paradise
As whispers in the wind
We glance at each other
But can't speak
Drifting in this dull lake

In no particular direction
Suddenly there is a ray of light
A lotus blooms in the lake
Wisdom reappears
In the dark underworld
Weaning away anger
From the angry men.

V
Here we walk in the dreary desert
Dreary desert, dreary desert
Here we walk in the dreary desert
All the three hundred and sixty-five days of the year

Between the talks
And the war
Between promises

And delivery
Revolves diplomacy
                    For ours is anger's dark underworld
Between cooperation
And coercion
Between demarche
And summon
Revolves diplomacy

                    For ours is anger's dark underworld
Between the doves
And the hawks
Between annihilation
And co-existence
Revolves diplomacy
                    For ours is anger's dark underworld
For us it is
To choose life or death
Survival or extinction

This is the way the world is saved
This is the way the world is saved
This is the way the world is saved
Not with wars but with diplomacy.

ABHAY K.

THE FIRE AND SERMON

After T.S. Eliot

The river's soul is slashed: its five fingers
Fractured and dammed with an imaginary border. The wind
Crosses back and forth the ancient land, unhindered. The saint has departed.
Sweet Indus, flow gently, till I sing again.
The river bears no blood stains, partition papers,
Silk flags, passports, blue or green
Or other remains of dark midnights. The saint has departed.
And their successors, the drifting souls of the subcontinent;
The departed have left only their words of wisdom.
By the lost waters of Sarasvati[1] I sit down and weep . . .
Sweet Indus, flow gently till I sing again,
Sweet Indus, flow gently, for I tread rough terrain.
I hear explosions in Pokhran[2]
The split of the atoms, shockwaves ripping the world apart.

Violent storms blew through the desert
Drowning villages and cities in sand
While I was strolling at Bandra bandstand
On a hot summer evening in Bombay
The desert shook again, this time in Quetta[3]

While I was grazing a cowherd in Balochistan
Dust rose in the sky turning the day into night
And the dry hot winds from the desert destroyed
All the sunflowers from Peshawar to Kanyakumari.
But from time to time I hear talks of sunflowers
Being revived or of planting a new crop of similar kind
Which will grow as fast and shine as bright.
O the sun shines bright in the desert
And there is no water
We drink only milk and eat only dessert
Sarve bhavantu sukhin, sarve santu niamayah
Sarve bhadrani pashyantu, ma kaschit dukh bhag bhavet! [4]

Ram Ram Sita Ram
Hare Krishna Hare Hare
Ishwar Allah Tero Nam
Sabko Sanmati De Bhagwan [5]

Eternal City
Under the smog of a November noon
Mrs. Kaul, the Civil Servant
Bright as ruby, in her finest Sari
Stitched in Benares by Banke Bihari,
Asked me gently in Hinglish
To dine at the India International Centre
Followed by a luminous night at a five-star hotel.

At the midnight hour, when the world sleeps
Turning and tossing in beds, when the humanity recuperates
Like a frog hibernating in winter,
I, Lord Mountbatten, though blind, swinging across the subcontinent,

Partitioned with a pen on paper, can see
At the midnight hour, the sun setting over the British Empire
Heading homeward, as the sailor returns home from sea,
It's teatime in London, time to make one's own breakfast, light
One's own stove, and to open canned tin food.
Of the vast empire
Over which the Sun never set,
What has been left?
Souvenirs, loot, kohinoor, and maps?
I, Mountbatten, now an old man with wrinkled skin
Foresaw what was coming, and left the scene—
All awaited that expected moment.
Nehru, the impatient man with the gift of gab, arrived,
The last Englishman, Macaulay's true son,
One of a kind the British could trust
Someone who could speak the language, a confidante.
The propitious hour arrived at midnight, as he agreed,
The Raj ended, India woke up from centuries of slumber,
for its tryst with destiny
but broken and limping.
Partitioned and bleeding, assaulted by invaders
and tribesmen heavily armed;
inviting immediate response,
that made a substantial difference.
(And I, the Time, have foreseen it all
Enacted on this same ancient land of Bharat;
I have fought in Kurukshetra and Karnal
And walked among the dead after the great war of Mahabharat.)
I Mountbatten deliver my final farewell speech,
And grope my way, after the sunset (on the Empire), to the sea . . .

India heaves a sigh of relief,
Fully aware of its new found freedom;
Its numb amputated body feels a streak of terror:
It must move on: now what's done is done.
When even great men stoop to folly and
Commit despicable acts partitioning the land
It wipes tears with its tender left hand,
And sobs silently alone at dawn.

A new music plays in the Moghul gardens
And along the Rajpath, up the Central Secretariat.
O Delhi o Delhi, I can sometimes hear
Beside a public monument at the India Gate,
The pleasant sounds of the common people's choir
And cooing and wooing
Of lovers under the moon: where the soldiers
Of India martyred in Mesopotamia, Persia, Flanders
East Africa, Gallipoli and France shine in splendor.

> The Yamuna drains
> Darkness
> From Delhi's soul
> With the downpour
> Of Monsoon
> In August
> Flooding parts of the city.
> The blood bath
> A sea of refugees
> At the Kingsway Camp
> Past the Delhi University.
> > *Waheguru, Waheguru*
> > *Ishwar Allah, Ishwar Allah*[6]

Men and women
Beating their chests
The boundary drawn
An imaginary line
In ink and blood
Spilled on paper
Rippled the lake
Monsoon wind
Carried across the subcontinent
The wails of children
Men and women
  Waheguru Waheguru
  Hare Krishna, Hare Ram

"*Sare Jahan Se Accha Hindostan Hamara.*
Hum Bulbule Hain Iski, Ye Gulsitan Hamara." [7]
Syed Ahmad Khan conceived a new Gulistan.
Iqbal sang a new Tarana and Jinnah undid me.

"My heart in Hindukush, and my feet in Arunachal
My hands stretched from Kashmir to Kanyakumari.
After the partition I cried. They promised a new dawn.
I kept silent. What could I say?"

"On Siachen Glacier.
I cannot link
Anything with anything.
The frostbitten bodies of my sons.
My humble sons who expect
Nothing."
 Ram Ram

To Rajghat[8] then I came and saw the saint

Burning burning burning burning

Hey Ram Hey Ram

Sabko Sanmati De Bhagwan.

NOTES

1. Sarasvati is a lost river in the Indian subcontinent.
2. Pokhran is a site in Rajasthan where nuclear tests were conducted.
3. Quetta is a site in Balochistan where nuclear experiments were conducted.
4. "May all be happy, may all look great, may there never be sorrow" is a thought from the Upanishads.
5. "Ishwar Allah Tero Nam . . ." is a popular prayer. It was recited by Mahatma Gandhi.
6. "Waheguru . . ." is a prayer chanted by the Sikhs and "Ishwar Allah and Hare Rama" by the Hindus.
7. "Sare Jahan se acchha . . . is a well-known poem written by poet Iqbal.
8. Rajghat is the final resting place of Mahatma Gandhi.

REVIEWED BY RICHARD MCCALLUM[1]

Abu-Nimer, Mohammed & Renáta Katalin Nelson, eds. 2021. *Evaluating Interreligious Peacebuilding and Dialogue: Methods and Frameworks.* Boston: De Gruyter.

I wish this book had been available in 2012 when I was first invited to evaluate the *Cambridge Interfaith Programme* Summer School.[2] When I looked for a framework to evaluate a simple interfaith encounter, I found virtually nothing. What I did find was in the field of non-religious conflict resolution and that in its infancy. The present volume with its focus on interreligious conflict resolution is one step closer to a serious consideration of interfaith evaluation more generally. It is a great contribution to the field bringing together as it does a wide range of experienced evaluators who discuss the theoretical underpinnings of evaluating interreligious peacebuilding, the tensions and politics between various stakeholders, as well as the practical methodology and tools available.

The volume has been published as part of an open access series, *Beyond Dialogue*, produced by the *King Abdullah bin Abdulaziz International Centre for Interreligious and Intercultural Dialogue* (KAICIID) which in 2021 moved from Vienna to Lisbon. Some in interfaith circles may be sceptical of an interfaith initiative launched by a Saudi king (d.2015) in a foreign land when the faiths cannot coexist in his own homeland. However that may be, this edited volume is a valuable publication and brings together some of the most experienced academics and practitioners in the field. Foremost amongst them is Professor Mohammed Abu-Nimer, now a senior advisor at KAICIID, who has been publishing on peacebuilding, non-violence in Islam and evaluation for over 20 years. This period covers the whole of the development of what this volume makes clear is a young, emerging field that has sprung up in the twenty-first century as a result of the pressing necessity to consider the role of religion and religious identity in conflicts around the world.

The book paints a picture of a field rapidly professionalising, developing resources and competing for funding. Peacemakers, evaluators and donors, religious or secular, will all find much help, wisdom and stimulation in its various chapters. Several of the authors discuss the lack of definitions and criteria for concepts such as "religious peacebuilding," "good results" and even what constitutes "peace" itself in any given context. Reina Neufeldt suggests that religious peacebuilding is "actions taken by individuals motivated by their religion or representing religious institutions to constructively and non-violently prevent, reduce or transform inter-group conflict" (p. 55). She goes on to discuss some of the theory and philosophical ideas that underpin it. Hippolyt Pul, writing in the African context, makes a strong case for the importance of listening to "those who have lived through conflict" as they are best placed to define these things and "know what best to call peace" (p. 96).

Many of the chapters include case studies, quotes from surveys and insights from interviews conducted with those in conflict situations. These helpfully ground the theoretical discussion, although maybe one could wish for more, as some of the chapters become a little repetitive, as is often the case with an edited volume of this nature. For instance, several of the chapters discuss the complex relationship between peacemaking practitioners, programme evaluators and donors, each of whom may have different priorities in the evaluation process. Whilst evaluators often favour a longitudinal approach and focus on the importance of learning, donors tend to work to a much shorter time frame and are interested in results, efficiency and accountability. Abu-Nimr interestingly notes that recent advances in technology have only fuelled the push for quick evaluations with quantifiable data (p. 26).

When it comes to methods and practical frameworks, there are maybe not as many as one might expect. There are no appendices with samples of surveys or interview schedules. There are few suggestions about how surveys should be constructed, interviews conducted, observations recorded or the role that journaling, video blogs and focus groups could play. The exception is the chapter by David Steele and the late Ricardo Wilson-Grau which provides several tables with sample questions demonstrating how data might be elicited to meet various evaluation goals. Otherwise, evaluators hoping for tools will need to build on the theory to create their own.

One of the most refreshing things about the volume is that it takes religious faith seriously. Of course, there is a danger that religion may be instrumentalised in the quest for peace and that religious leaders may be co-opted for political ends but still religion is not seen as necessarily a bad thing. Pul does warn against an over-focus on religion which may risk losing sight of other root political, ethnic or economic causes. He points out that particularly in Africa "religious identities are fluid" and "hybrid" (pp. 84–5), particularly when it comes to "exogenous religions" such as Christianity and Islam. However, Steele & Wilson-Gau highlight the importance of recognising the place of transcendence and the supernatural in many contexts, meaning that the values, motivations and measures of religious peacebuilders may not be the same as those of secular evaluators. Khaled Ehsan focuses on the power dynamics of religious leadership and provides brief case studies from contexts as diverse as Afghanistan, Nigeria and the USA to explore the potential for and limitations on religious leaders involved in peacemaking.

The final chapter by Shana Cohen is rather different in that it focuses not on the evaluation of a particular event or programme, nor indeed on interreligious peacemaking. Rather it focuses on evaluating interfaith more generally as a field. To do this it focuses on the UK and makes the observation that, whilst interfaith activity understandably peaked in the wake of the attacks on New York in September 2001 and London in 2005, it has since declined. Cohen suggests that there are various reasons for this including: "cynicism or wariness concerning the impact of explicitly interfaith initiatives" (p. 202); a lack of funding due to austerity; changes in government policy further reducing funding; and the change in *Church of England* leadership from Rowan Williams to Justin Welby. This last hypothesis seems rather unfair in the light of Welby's focus on reconciliation as one of his three personal priorities.[3] However, maybe more pertinent, she believes that a younger generation is interested not so much in the theological aspect of interfaith but rather in its potential for collaboration in social action, such as cleaning up local parks together. Indeed, she remarks that "organizers were frank in their desire not to discuss religion" (p. 207). This is all well and good, but it risks building community relationships on the shaky foundation of assumption and wishful thinking on all sides.

The content of faith must surely remain important and open to rigorous question. This is why Neufeldt's "theological dialogue" is still such an important undertaking alongside "political" and "peacebuilding" dialogues (p. 63). How are texts, interpretative histories and modern hermeneutics to be factored into any evaluation of interreligious peacemaking? Garred, Herrington and Hume point out the frustration amongst those working in the field with an assumption by policy makers trying to counter or prevent violent extremism (C/PVE) that "religion is more of a driver of conflict than it is of peace" with Islam being the "most problematic" (p. 187). A recognition by the contributors that religion and transcendence can play a positive role in peacemaking is very welcome but needs to be balanced with a willingness to engage with the diverse intricacies, and even the darker sides, of all religious traditions. Whilst there are undoubtedly many and complex causes of religious conflict, theology remains one of them and should not be ignored in the evaluation process.

NOTES

1. An earlier version of this review was posted at: https://www.cmcsoxford.org.uk/resources/book-reviews/interreligious-peacemaking
2. McCallum, Richard. 2018. "Towards a framework and methodology for the evaluation of inter-faith initiatives" and "Evaluating Inter-faith Initiatives: A Cambridge case study," *Studies in Interreligious Dialogue*, 27.1: 63-103.
3. https://www.archbishopofcanterbury.org/priorities/reconciliation

NOTES ON RECENT BOOKS IN RELIGION AND DIPLOMACY

Sherrie M. Steiner and James T. Christie, eds. *Religious Soft Diplomacy and the United Nations: Religious Engagement as Loyal Opposition*. 2021. Lanham, MD: Lexington Books. 372pp.

Contributions by Sherrie M. Steiner, James T. Christie, Brian Adams, Alvaro Albacete, Keith Best, William Alexander Blaikie, Rachel Blaney, Ganoune Diop, Adis Duderija, Leah Gazan, Cesar Jaramillo, Azza Karam, Christine Macmillan, Steven Moore, Paul Morris, Peter Noteboom, and Upolu Luma Vaai

In the prologue to this collection, Alvaro Albacete suggests that both "religion" and "diplomacy" have mutual aims in that they both seek peace and stability. They both have the capabilities to aid in human development by mobilizing local communities and creating social cohesions. Of course, each side has the capabilities of manipulating the other side, and some peaceful co-working is often not an easy goal to achieve.

Contributions examine these tensions from multiple specific issues, centered around the United Nations, and including Canadian culture wars, women's rights in Islamic societies, police brutality, climate change, and the importance of religious dissent. Overall, these contributions create a strong argument that the United Nations will need to shift their understanding of how religious systems operate in order to bring about better social cohesion.

Victor Gaetan. *God's Diplomats: Pope Francis, Vatican Diplomacy, and America's Armageddon*. 2021. Lanham, MD: Rowman & Littlefield Publishers. 476pp.

While the pope does not command an army of any significance, he has a diplomatic corps that plays in the highest league of global diplomacy. From the Cold War to all major current conflicts, the Vatican engages in official and unofficial diplomatic activities which are not predetermined by alliances but follow the Catholic leadership's own reasoning. Some of these activities have caused significant headaches to the U.S. administration, such as when in 1989 Panama's toppled leader Manuel Noriega sought asylum in the Apostolic Nuntiature to avoid capture by U.S. forces, or when popes oppose specific wars, such as the bombing raids on North Vietnam or the invasion of Iraq.

Part I of *God's Diplomats* offers a wide range of insights into the Vatican's mission beyond religion and the people who often wear "multiple mitres"—having to fulfill religious and diplomatic functions in their roles. Part II illuminates the diplomacy of Pope Francis, which is marked by three characteristics: commitment to personal encounters, respect for local perception, and patience. Each of the seven short chapters in this part focuses on a specific geographical setting from Ukraine to Kenya to the Middle East to South Sudan.

Sarah Wolff. *Secular Power Europe and Islam: Identity and Foreign Policy*. 2021. Ann Arbor, MI: University of Michigan Press. 198pp.

Sarah Wolff explores the EU's engagement with Islam and more generally how secularism drives the EU's relation to religion. The study is based on interviews with policy makers, civil society representatives, and think tank participants as well as participant observation and an analysis of a wide range of documents. In EU contexts, engaging religion and interreligious dialogue often serves security purposes by seeking to moderate and regulate Islam and especially containing "radical" Islam that could be a source of instability both within the EU and for EU friendly regimes. When diplomats receive training on religion as part of EU and European foreign policy training, it is from a perspective of the "other," thereby stabilizing the EU's identity as a secular-liberal power.

Wolff argues that secularism is not the neutral bedrock of international relations that it is sometimes taken to be, but one worldview among many others that shape EU foreign policy. As a quote by Franco-Lebanese novelist Amin Maalouf indicates, no worldview, doctrine, or religion is in itself necessarily a liberating force, and the same holds true for secularism. Wolff shows how the EU's response to Islam can be understood better if it is seen in the context of the EU's existential anxieties about its security and identity.

The book offers three case studies: the first focuses on the EU's diplomatic practices regarding Islam, the second on the interest of diplomats in religious engagement, and the third on the issue of blasphemy and freedom of religion or belief.

Philip McDonagh, Kishan Manocha, John Neary, and Lucia Vázquez Mendoza. *On the Significance of Religion for Global Diplomacy.* **2021. London: Routledge. 182pp.**

Addressing academics, religious actors, and policy makers, *On the Significance of Religion for Global Diplomacy* makes the case for a more creative global diplomacy that welcomes contributions from religious representatives and religious perspectives. Multilateral actors like the UN, the Organization for Security and Cooperation in Europe (OSCE) and the European Union should work towards a culture of encounter that includes the world's religious traditions, not just to be more inclusive but to make these organizations more fit-for-purpose and to enable them to meet the pressing global challenges from climate change to widening social disparities.

The book's aim is to (re)introduce some deep and fundamental questions into the sphere of multilateral diplomacy, like "What do we believe in? What is our 'design for living'?" At the same time, the approach is practice oriented and offers recommendations for those working in the field of religion and diplomacy. For example, the civilizations of the Axial Age are said to have shared a number of conceptions about the nature of peace which can also contribute today to the task of finding and sustaining shared values and the vocabulary to speak about them. In the epilogue, the idea of an Agora for Europe as an all-European initiative is developed as illustration of how such recommendations could be implemented in a concrete initiative.

Evan Berry, ed. *Climate Politics and the Power of Religion.* **2022. Bloomington, IN: Indiana University Press. 298pp.**

> **Contributions by** Andrew Thompson, Ken Conca, David T. Buckley, Kelly D. Alley, Ana Mariella Bacigalupo, Roger-Mark De Souza, Neeraj Vedwan, and J. Brent Crosson.

Religious communities around the world face the challenge of coming to terms with the sometimes devastating effects of climate change. This volume is the outcome of a research project "Religion and Climate Change in Cross-Regional Perspective," which included, as one of three project streams, a focus on the significance of religious actors such as religious leaders and faith-based organizations.

Climate Politics and the Power of Religion shows the often novel and experimental ways in which religious communities respond to environmental pressures. It seeks to balance a secular bias in environmental politics by showing that in many geographical contexts, religion plays an important role in public discussions about climate change, that religion impacts on the national level of climate policy, and that these religious elements are "refracted" into multilateral policy contexts and international climate diplomacy.

CONTRIBUTORS

Melanie Barbato is a researcher at the University of Münster, Germany and Oxford Centre for Hindu Studies, UK. Her current project looks at dialogue and diplomacy in the Vatican's and World Council of Churches' involvement in Hindu-Christian relations. Her book *Jain Approaches to Plurality* (2017) was published by Brill in the series Currents of Encounter. www.melaniebarbato.com

Michael Daniel Driessen is Associate Professor of the Department of Political Science and International Affairs at John Cabot University, Rome. He received his doctorate from the University of Notre Dame and has been a post-doctoral fellow at Georgetown University's School of Foreign Service in Doha, Qatar as well as a Jean Monnet Fellow at the European University Institute in Florence. He has published the book *Religion and Democratization* (Oxford University Press, 2014), and his articles have appeared in *Comparative Politics, Sociology of Religion, Politics and Religion,* and *Democratization.* His new book, "The Global Politics of Interreligious Dialogue" is forthcoming with Oxford University Press. Michael also serves as an advisor for the *Adyan* Foundation in Lebanon with whom he has published a number of policy reports.

Pasquale Ferrara is General Director for Political and Security Affairs at the Italian Ministry of Foreign Affairs. He was previously Italy's Special Envoy for Libya. Between October 2106 to November 2020, he served as Italian Ambassador in Algeria. Since 1984, he engaged in both bilateral and multilateral diplomacy, having served in the US, Brussels (EU), Greece and Chile. As Director of the Policy Planning at the Italian MFA, he launched a new program on Religion and International Relations. He teaches Diplomacy and Negotiation at LUISS University in Rome.

Abhay K. is the author of ten poetry books including *Monsoon* (Sahitya Akademi, 2022), *The Magic of Madagascar* (L'Harmattan Paris, 2021), *The Alphabets of Latin America* (Bloomsbury India, 2020), and the editor of *The Bloomsbury Book of Great Indian Love Poems, CAPITALS, New Brazilian Poems,* and *The Bloomsbury Anthology of Great Indian Poems.* His poems have appeared in over 100 literary magazines including *Poetry Salzburg Review, Asia Literary Review* among others.

His 'Earth Anthem' has been translated into over 150 languages. He has received SAARC Literary Award 2013 and was invited to record his poems at the Library of Congress, Washington, D.C. in 2018. His translations of Kalidasa's *Meghaduta* (Bloomsbury India, 2021) and *Ritusamhara* (Bloomsbury India, 2021) from Sanskrit won KLF Poetry Book of the Year Award 2020-21. www.abhayk.com

Sharon Rosen is Director of Religious Engagement globally at the international peacebuilding organization Search for Common Ground. An expert on designing and implementing interreligious programming that builds collaboration across religions and promotes peace, she co-founded the *Universal Code of Conduct on Holy Sites*, led the development of the *Common Ground Approach to Religious Engagement* toolkit, and co-created a seminal online course with the United States Institute of Peace on *Religious Engagement in Peacebuilding—A Common Ground Approach*.

Nukhet Sandal is an Associate Professor of Political Science and an Associate Dean at the College of Arts and Sciences at Ohio University. She is the Editor-in-Chief of the *Oxford Research Encyclopedia of International Studies*. She is the author of *Religious Leaders and Conflict Transformation* (Cambridge University Press, 2017) and *Religion and International Relations Theory* (with Jonathan Fox; Routledge, 2013), and the editor of *Religion and Peace: Global Perspectives and Possibilities* (with Ingo Trauschweizer; Ohio University Press, 2022).

Juyan Zhang is a professor at the University of Texas at San Antonio and Contributing Scholar of Faith Diplomacy for the USC Center on Public Diplomacy. His research focuses on public diplomacy and strategic communication. He has also published in the field of Buddhist studies.

www.ingramcontent.com/pod-product-compliance
Lightning Source LLC
Chambersburg PA
CBHW040259170426
43193CB00020B/2950